CHINESE POSTERS

Art from the Great Proletarian Cultural Revolution

Lincoln Cushing and Ann Tompkins

CHRONICLE BOOKS
SAN FRANCISCO

All poster reproductions in this book were shot by Lincoln Cushing, from the Ann Tompkins (Tang Fandi) and Lincoln Cushing Chinese Poster Collection, East Asian Library, U.C. Berkeley, with these exceptions, all found on page 16: Concrete Foundation of the Arts original poster courtesy AOUON Archive, with permission of Pat Ryan; *News from Neasden* booklet cover from Lincoln Cushing personal archive, with permission of Clifford Harper, www.agraphia.uk.com; "Freedom of the Press" graphic image provided courtesy of Kirk Anderson, www.kirktoons.com. Photographs are credited in captions.

Library of Congress Cataloging-in-Publication Data:

Cushing, Lincoln, 1953–
Chinese posters : Art from the great proletarian cultural revolution / by Lincoln Cushing and Ann Tompkins.
    p. cm.
Includes bibliographical references and index.
ISBN-13: 978-0-8118-5946-2
ISBN-10: 0-8118-5946-0
1. China—History—Cultural Revolution, 1966–1976
Art and the revolution.
2. China—History—Cultural Revolution, 1966–1976
Posters. I. Tompkins, Ann . II. Title.

DS778.7C87 2007
741.6'74095109046—dc22
2007010993

Manufactured in Hong Kong
Designed by Distinc

Distributed in Canada by Raincoast Books
9050 Shaughnessy Street
Vancouver, British Columbia V6P 6E5

10 9 8 7 6 5 4 3 2 1

Chronicle Books LLC
680 Second Street
San Francisco, California 94107
www.chroniclebooks.com

A note on spellings and translations

The transliteration of Chinese to English is an imperfect art. The first challenge lies in representing the phonetic sounds of the Chinese national standard language (often called Mandarin outside of China) in a roman alphabet. For many years the dominant method for representing Chinese in English was the Wade-Giles system, giving us such spellings as "Kuomintang" (resulting in the abbreviation of KMT) and "Mao Tse-tung." In 1958 a system called Pinyin (meaning "fixed sound") was developed after extensive study with consideration of many foreign languages, which produced spellings that were more phonetically accurate: "Guomindang," "Mao Zedong." Adoption of Pinyin has been slow among many anticommunist Chinese diaspora communities because it was instituted by the People's Republic of China. These alternate transliteration approaches have resulted in terms being spelled two or more ways in the literature and on the posters. The convention in this book is to use Pinyin unless it appears in a phrase or title that uses a Wade-Giles term.

The second challenge, concerning phrases such as poster titles, is that some terms simply do not translate into English that reads well and makes sense. There is no one correct way to present them, given the wide disparity between Chinese and English syntax and grammar. In Chinese, for example, many nouns are ambiguously singular or plural. Some political phrases ("proletarians of the world" or "peoples of the world") may seem clumsy or dated to today's reader, and some terms have nuances that are awkward to explain in the short format of a title. This is why the same poster in another book may have a title reflecting a different interpretation.

Contents

Introduction

The posters in this book were produced during the Great Proletarian Cultural Revolution (GPCR), a period roughly spanning the years from 1966 to 1976. This was an incredibly tumultuous period in Chinese history, an epic struggle within the Chinese Communist Party (CCP) that was taken to the citizens to determine the country's future. It was but one in a long series of campaigns and events undertaken by the CCP that depended on massive popular support and was designed to bring progress to a huge, poor, rural country that had only recently emerged from feudalism and foreign domination. Through a public organizing method known in China as "from the masses, to the masses," millions of Chinese people were mobilized to solve a wide variety of problems, from how to win wars to campaigns on public policies. The latter included mass mobilizations to end bureaucratic corruption and waste; improve public health; expand literacy and Marxist study; and develop cooperatives, communes, and state-owned farms. "The masses" were even involved in certain efforts within the CCP to clarify and strengthen political policies and "clean the ranks" of the organization. The movements had successes and shortcomings, some with errors having serious consequences. Overlaying these mass movements was an ideological division within the CCP about the right way to implement revolutionary ideals and about whether there could be a restoration of capitalism when a communist party was in power. Actions and ideas that were considered counter to accepted Marxist theory were criticized by both sides as "revisionist" in the ongoing argument about the direction of the party and Chinese society. This conflict was not only a debate within the CCP, but also within and among the Communist Parties worldwide, and it was also at the root of the GPCR.

The GPCR is one of the most controversial and charged subjects in twentieth-century political history. This book is about one aspect of this period, the posters made during and soon after the GPCR, and so we as authors have refrained from undertaking a full analysis of the GPCR. We have also made every effort to avoid stating the unsupportable, and to present enough contextual definitions and information to help the reader understand these remarkable posters.

The Great Proletarian Cultural Revolution

From 1921 to 1949, armies within China fought two civil wars and a war to oppose foreign aggression. After 1949, when the CCP-led forces established the government of the People's Republic of China, the armed struggle ended, but there were still constant contests between ideologies and activities seen as serving the interests of the bourgeoisie (private owning class) or the proletarians (working people).

The immediate precursor of the political struggles of the GPCR was the Great Leap Forward (GLF, 1958–1960), an ambitious five-year plan to modernize China, boost its gross national product, and increase the pace of Chinese socialist transformation. The CCP's policies called for a massive restructuring of China's agricultural and industrial production into localized collectives, with major efforts to increase output in agriculture, iron smelting and steel refining, coal production, and water control projects. However, natural disasters coincided with poor planning and the abrupt withdrawal of Soviet aid and technical advisors, which contributed to widespread famines that resulted in major setbacks and a huge death toll (the precise number is the subject of heated debate, in part due to a dearth of complete and accurate records). In the aftermath, Mao Zedong stepped aside as head of state while continuing as Chairman of the Communist Party, and state leadership was taken up by President Liu Shaoqi, with Premier Zhou Enlai and CCP General Secretary Deng Xiaoping taking on a more active role in government. The shift in leadership resulted in the implementation of new policies—a shift away from the primacy of the commune and reinstatement of private ownership of land, free markets, and small business—which were considered by others in the Party, notably including Mao Zedong, as undermining the revolutionary ideal of a classless society. This fundamental difference about how the Chinese revolution should proceed was expressed as two "lines"—contrasting political policies that would lead to different outcomes—and was referred to during the GPCR as "taking the socialist road or the capitalist road."

On May 16, 1966, in what many regard as the official starting point of the GPCR, the CCP's Central Committee published a document that provided the "theory, line, principles, and policies for continuing the revolution under the dictatorship of the proletariat." At the same time, the Central Committee dismissed the Cultural Revolution Group, which had been established two years earlier to lead criticism of corrupt and bourgeois tendencies among academics and bureaucrats but was now seen as acting contrary to cultural reforms supported by Mao Zedong. The Central Committee replaced it with the Cultural Revolution Small Group, with Jiang Qing (Politburo member and Mao Zedong's wife) serving as deputy director. Chen Boda, Chairman Mao's former political secretary, also served in the group. A wave of public debate and criticism of various government policies ensued across the country, played out on the pages of the *People's Daily* and other newspapers, as well as by means of big character posters, or *dazibao*. On August 5, Mao wrote his own *dazibao* at Beijing University, calling on the people to "Bombard the Headquarters" (meaning to criticize counterrevolutionary activity in the top levels of the CCP). This resulted in extensive public involvement in the struggle for the direction of the Party and the country. A few days later, on August 8,

the CCP Central Committee issued a sixteen-point set of guidelines for the movement. It was at this time that the Red Guards (primarily composed of students, but also including workers, peasants, and others) emerged and quickly developed as a mass movement to challenge counterrevolutionary and revisionist activity.

The Red Guards participated in a range of activities, including political education and *dazibao* debates; military training; physical fitness; the arts; efforts to assure proletarian control of educational, work, and government units; and public criticism and denunciations of perceived revisionists and class enemies. In practice, the various groups of the Red Guards did not consistently represent either line in the two-line struggle, but incorporated many tendencies, all proclaiming that they were supporting "the socialist road" for China. In 1967, fighting among Red Guard factions in some locations led to the intercession of the People's Liberation Army (PLA).

Throughout these years, Mao's ideal of a society directed by and serving the masses was widely embraced. The People's Liberation Army had a long history of political study within its ranks, and Defense Minister Lin Biao organized some of Mao's writings into book form as *Quotations from Chairman Mao Tse-tung* (also known in the West as the "Little Red Book"). First published in 1964, the book became widely used in study sessions in China's schools, workplaces, and neighborhoods, and around the world. In 1968, Chairman Mao and Premier Zhou Enlai called on students and young people to go to the countryside to learn from the peasants and the poor and to assist with literacy education and other technical skills. The power struggles within the Party led to the expulsion of President Liu Shaoqi (who died in prison), the posthumous condemnation of Lin Biao (suspected of plotting against Mao, he reportedly died in a plane crash en route to the USSR), and the ouster and later return to key leadership role of Deng

Xiaoping. After Mao Zedong's death in 1976 and after the arrest and trial of ten Communist Party leaders (including Jiang Qing and others known as "The Gang of Four"), all of whom were blamed by the 1981 leadership for excesses during the Cultural Revolution, the GPCR lost its key proponents in the CCP leadership. The GPCR was officially declared over in 1977 by the Eleventh Party Congress, and Liu Shaoqi and his policies were officially rehabilitated. In 1981, the CCP repudiated the GPCR, placing responsibility for it on Mao Zedong, a position regarded by many scholars as an over simplification of a complex historical period. China continues to grapple with the challenges of building socialism within a predominantly capitalist world, a world in which change is the only constant.

Revolutionary Chinese Posters and Their Impact Abroad by Lincoln Cushing

Artwork in China During the GPCR

China has the oldest printmaking history in the world, a vibrant tradition centuries before Gutenberg developed the groundbreaking concept of movable type. Woodblock prints were invented during the Tang dynasty (A.D. 618–907), allowing art to be mechanically duplicated for the first time. Later, some mass-produced documents addressed social change movements, such as the illustrated tracts and leaflets created during the 1900 Boxer Rebellion to oppose European cultural penetration. But modern Chinese posters, used as a means of mass communication, are a relatively recent genre that evolved into a distinct form under the direction of the Chinese Communist Party (CCP). These propaganda posters were mounted in public places and sold in stores. Like public art in the later stages of the postrevolutionary Soviet Union, these posters fell under the principle that art and literature must serve the people. Mao Zedong formally articulated this position even before the Chinese Communist revolution had succeeded:

> Revolutionary culture is a powerful revolutionary weapon for the broad masses of the people. It prepares the ground ideologically before the revolution comes and is an important, indeed essential, fighting front in the general revolutionary front during the revolution.
>
> *On New Democracy*, January 1940 [1]

> Our literary and art workers must accomplish [their] task and shift their stand; they must gradually move their feet over to the side of the workers, peasants, and soldiers, to the side of the proletariat, through the process of going into their very midst and into the thick of practical struggles and through the process of studying Marxism and society.
>
> *Talks at the Yanan Forum on Literature and Art*, May 1942 [2]

During the GPCR, the arts, including posters, were defined by several guiding political principles:

1. **Rejection of Western and classical Chinese styles.** The GPCR sought to build a new socialist nation without reliance on the values of foreign societies or previous corrupt domestic ones. This meant striving to create new, modern Chinese forms. Although the general style of Socialist Realist propaganda art was adopted from the Soviet Union and taught in most of the Chinese art schools, the Chinese worked to make the art and rhetoric uniquely their own.

2. **Developing artwork from previously disenfranchised social strata and regions.** Formally trained artists were thought likely to harbor revisionist values (ones not supportive of fundamental class struggle), and a huge effort went into finding and supporting art by people who were workers, peasants, and soldiers. To a more limited degree, the GPCR encouraged art about and by ethnic minorities.

3. **Rejection of "art for art's sake."** Art styles narrowed to a slim range of Socialist Realism,[3] without abstraction or modernism. Art was expected to have some sort of productive social function or application. Artists did not sign their work, though most did get individual or collective published credit.

Some scholars have described the GPCR as representing a "lost chapter" of Chinese art history because of the narrow range of officially accepted forms and the view that Party politics trumped artistic creativity. There are numerous examples of artwork destroyed, academic departments dismantled, personal careers ruined, and even imprisonment and death.[4] Yet there are alternate views of the GPCR that recognize some

---

1 *Quotations from Chairman Mao Tse-tung* (first English edition, 1966), 199.

2 Ibid., 300.

3 "In 1932, Joseph Stalin decreed Socialist Realism as the official art of the USSR, a diktat that led to Stalinist control over all artistic production. The aim of Socialist Realism was to pro-

duce realistic works that not only extolled workers and the glories of communism, but called attention to the wisdom of the Communist Party and its leadership." Mark Vallen, "The Shabbiness of Today's Art Criticism" *Art for a Change*, July 1, 2006; www.art-for-a-change.com/blog/2006_07_01_archive.html.

of its positive contributions to art and culture, especially within the complicated trajectory of the Chinese revolution and its deep-seated class antagonisms. In spirit, many of these goals were laudable. For example, many countries struggle to keep their domestic arts production from being overwhelmed by foreign commercial media culture; even a modern Western democracy such as Canada has a national radio broadcast policy requiring that a percentage of its content be generated domestically. The state-sponsored encouragement of artmaking by ordinary citizens is a democratic ideal, one fostered in the United States during the 1930s by the Works Progress Administration's Federal Art Project. And the concept that art should not be divorced from social needs and practice is a matter of long-standing debate within the art world, one hardly unique to the GPCR.

Academic studies in this field are still rare, and given the polarized nature of the issues it is assured that future analysis will continue to be characterized by many differences of opinion.

Media Institutions and Processes

In the period between the founding of the People's Republic of China in 1949 and the GPCR, propaganda policies were set by the CCP Central Committee and the Propaganda Department of the CCP. These policies were implemented vertically through an extensive hierarchical network at different administrative and provincial levels, as well as horizontally through mass organizations such as women's and trade union organizations. In May of 1966, the Propaganda Department was replaced with the Cultural Revolution Small Group under the control of Jiang Qing. Her background in theater guided the visual styles evident in cultural work in most genres, including poster art, throughout the GPCR. The ideological basis for "The Eight Model Works" (the main operas or ballets promoted by the State during the GPCR) followed narrow guidelines:

> On the basis of her "Three Prominences" (stress positive characters, the heroic in them, and stress the most central of the main characters) the subjects were portrayed realistically; and, by employing the techniques of mise en scène, the subjects were always in the centre of the action, flooded with light from the sun or from hidden sources. The themes that were addressed included the victories of the Cultural Revolution; heroic images of workers, peasants, and soldiers; successes in industry and agriculture, etcetera.[5]

This vision, coupled with the Soviet-influenced painting style embraced by the art colleges, resulted in a very formulaic and tightly defined visual style, even prescribing color choices and techniques:

> It was widely accepted among Cultural Revolution–era artists that images of Mao should be "red, smooth, and luminescent." Many of these conventions were developed during the Red Guard art movement and go beyond any oil-painting conventions imported from the Soviet Union. While Soviet socialist realism is still the most evident stylistic source for such compositions, details of color and texture may also be related to the more elegant of preliberation New Year's pictures. Cool colors were to be avoided; Mao's flesh should be modeled in red and other warm tones. Conspicuous displays of brushwork should not be seen; Mao's face should be smooth in appearance. The entire composition should be bright, and should be illuminated in such a way as to imply that Mao himself was the primary source of light. If Mao were in the center of a group of people, all surfaces that faced him should appear to be illuminated. In this way,

4   "During the trial [of Jiang Qing] the state asserted that 34,800 had been persecuted to death during the Cultural Revolution." Scott Watson, "The Total Art of Mao Zedong," *Art of the Great Proletarian Cultural Revolution 1966–1976* (Toronto: Morris and Helen Belkin Art Gallery, 2002), 7.

5   Stefan Landsberger, *Chinese Propaganda Posters: From Revolution to Modernization* (Amsterdam: Pepin Press, 1995), 41.

slogans such as "Mao is the sun in our hearts" could be made tangible.[6]

Although most of the posters were generated through the CCP and its propaganda units, many others were produced directly by Red Guards acting independently. The group responsible for generating Red Guard propaganda was the Revolutionary Rebel Corps, the GPCR name for the provincial branches of the All-China Federation of Literary and Arts Circles founded in 1949.

> The new propaganda publications, not surprisingly, bypassed regular pre–Cultural Revolution dissemination procedures. Rather than working with a publisher, the Red Guard artists simply took their artwork to the printing factory, which produced it at cost, as an act of patriotism. The Red Guard then distributed their product nationally.[7]

True understanding of the messages of these posters during this period is extremely challenging, because they refer to political issues that were often short-lived and, to outsiders, obscure. For example, Mao's major campaign in 1973 against the teachings of Confucius was really designed to challenge the authority of Lin Biao during the period of discord between the two. Minor details such as the arrangement of figures, the presence or absence of individuals, and the choice of text or color could often contribute significant political nuance to the visual message.

> In the latter phase of the GPCR and afterward, Zhou Enlai articulated an approach to cultural production quite different from that of Jiang Qing as part of a strategy attuned to foreign visitors to the PRC. Subjects such as natural landscapes, traditional history, and European culture appeared, as did a broader range of styles—even abstraction.

> Zhou Enlai, always sensitive to China's world image, requested in 1971 that the hotels and railway stations defaced by Red Guard slogans and pictures be redecorated. The foreign visitors who were invited to China during the diplomatic thaw of the 1970s were to be shown an elegant, orderly image. The paintings should be in national, contemporary styles. They were to display China's ancient cultural history and artistic standards and to be both simple and bold. For these purposes, landscape painting was not to be considered one of the 'four olds.' Similar works were to be prepared for export, to earn needed foreign exchange.[8]

The Specific Role of Posters

Political posters anywhere in the world can be generally divided into two distinct categories: those produced within the dominant system (the state, business interests, and so on) and those that challenge it (sometimes called "oppositional" art). The posters in this book clearly belong to the first category. With few exceptions, they were part of a comprehensive and highly controlled media apparatus whose objectives were the consolidation of authority and the transformation of society under a particular model. Thus they are similar to posters produced by the United States government during the Second World War, and posters from the Soviet Union and Cuba after their respective revolutions. Visually, the Chinese posters form a distinct subgenre because of their consistent style—full-color reproductions of painted or woodcut Socialist Realist art matched with bold, emphatic slogans. One unique characteristic of these posters is their embedded metadata, a cataloging-in-print system among the most thorough and consistent in the world. Almost every poster includes several lines of tiny type that describe numerous fields of information, including sale price, artist, printing facility, publisher, print run, edition, edition year, and item code.

6 Julia F. Andrews, *Painters and Politics in the People's Republic of China, 1949–1979* (Berkeley: University of California Press/Center for Chinese Studies, University of Michigan, 1994), 360.

7 Ibid., 324.

8 Ibid, 368.

Posters as a propaganda genre appeared in several different forms during the GPCR. Despite educational advances achieved after the revolution, few people in this largely rural country could read or write. According to published statistics of the China National Census, the rate of illiteracy in 1964 was just over 57 percent, considerably improved from the 80 percent rate in 1949,[9] but nonetheless a limiting factor for the influence of print media, with the exception of items that relied on small amounts of text and were reinforced by visual content. This created a fertile environment for posters as a medium.

There were many types of posters produced in China during this period, the two main genres being character posters (*dazibao*) and "commercial" posters with artwork. Although posters identical in concept to the *dazibao*—also known as the wall poster or big-character poster—were a central feature of news dissemination after the Russian revolution, the medium was employed on a massively larger scale in China. Many were a form of handmade popular expression, with no fixed format or style (they did not even need to be on paper—some were chalked on floors), and could include graphics (pictures with text were called *meishu dazibao*), slogans, puns, poems, commentary, and personal opinions. *Dazibao* were vital to Mao's struggle during the GPCR.

Although most *dazibao* were freely created and posted on walls in large and mid-size cities, in factories, and in communes, others went through a formal review process, involving submission to an editorial board, which could result in production and national dissemination. One example of public criticism distinctions was that press criticism of people *by name* was supposed to require Party committee review.[10] There were also small-character posters *(xiaozibao),* which occupied an important stratum of the media continuum. These covered much the same content, but were written in pen or pencil on small sheets of paper and posted on bulletin boards in virtually every work unit.

The prints in this book, with the exception of the few independently printed ones, differ from character posters in that they are "commercial" posters. They prominently featured artwork, and they were offset printed in large editions at state presses and produced as government propaganda to be sold in stores. They were very inexpensive—some were as little as .03 yuan (3 fen, or 3 Chinese cents) and most cost 11 to 32 fen.

The Chinese have a tradition of decorating their homes during big festivals—for example, the Chinese Lunar New Year, the National Day, or an important gathering for ancestor worship. In the old days people would buy paper cuts or traditional paintings of gods and a lot of folk art—paintings, posters. This was part of Chinese culture for many centuries. But things changed dramatically after 1966. . . . All these paintings—called traditional Chinese paintings—were labeled "feudalist" and were banned. Nobody could produce them. They were treated as evil, belonging to the old society. So when people wanted to decorate their homes they could only have proletarian artworks. These posters were the only remaining visual art of any kind that was available to ordinary people.

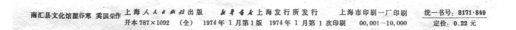

9 China's Fifth National Census, 2000. www.iiz-dvv.de/ englisch/ Publikationen/Ewb_ausgaben/60_2003/eng_xieguodong.htm.
10 "Point 11: The Question of Criticizing by Name in the Press," *Decision of the Central Committee of the Chinese Communist Party Concerning the Great Proletarian Cultural Revolution* (Beijing: Foreign Languages Press, 1966), 10.

An example of published poster data, enlarged for legibility [from poster on page 52 top right].

During the festivals and holidays, when you went to the market, you could see these posters. Mostly they were sold in what was called the "New China Bookstore," a national chain—sort of like our Borders, or Barnes & Noble, but much larger—the only bookstore in the country, run by the government. All major cities and townships had them. The stores had a section of posters [where] you could go and pick up whatever you liked. Of course, these were proletarian art, sold as commercial commodities, but they also had a political purpose. They were supposed to educate the masses, to convey the Party's policy and Mao Zedong's thought, but they were also beautiful artwork. In the country, there were many art schools during the GPCR that did nothing but produce those propaganda posters. Propaganda was not a bad word in those days. These were a part of everyone's life in that period.[11]

Most of these posters were intended for consumption within China, but a small number of titles were designed for export. These were printed on a slightly heavier paper and had text in foreign languages, usually English, French, and German. There is evidence that the posters for foreign distribution followed a distinct production path; they lack the same detailed metadata credits found on the domestic posters, and many are instead identified with a series code, "86 CEFG," followed by a three-digit number.

The artworks produced for these posters were called *xuanchuanhua* (propaganda pictures or images), a term that can apply to other media such as cartoons. Although there was much encouragement during the GPCR to develop and use artwork by amateurs, in many cases uncredited trained professionals were involved.

The inherent contradiction between the technically weak but politically correct entries of workers, peasants, and soldiers on the one

Women's shock brigade.
Artist unknown; published by Shanghai
People's Publishing House, 1975.
53 x 77 cm

11 Peter Zhou, director of the East Asian Library at U.C. Berkeley.
Interview by Lincoln Cushing, July 2006.

hand, and the propaganda institution director Gao Jingde's mandate to seek high standards on the other, was resolved by forming "painting correction groups." In this system, a prominent young oil painting professional accompanied the paintings submitted by each major geographic region when they were shipped to the capital. When an amateur work that might have interesting subject matter but was poorly painted was criticized by jury members, officials, and other artists, the professional from the artist's own region would "correct" it, simply repainting problematic sections. If the officials still found the work inadequate, artists from other regions might complete the repainting.[12]

Visual Genres and Recurrent Iconography

The posters in this book represent some of the visual styles and themes that were produced in China during the GPCR. In analyzing them, it is important to distinguish between the graphic design of the poster—the composition, typography, shape, and other factors—and the artwork in the poster. From a design point of view, the vast majority of these posters are very stylistically consistent, composed of a dominant representational image (reproduced from a woodcut or an oil or watercolor painting) to which a graphic designer has added a headline and a secondary level of text. The typography is very simple and unimaginative, certainly when compared to the wild experimentation with letterforms elsewhere at the time, such as U.S. rock or Cuban posters. There are several possible reasons for this, including the serious nature of the political task, but technology may have also played a role. Most Chinese printing presses were still using lead type, and designers probably did not have access to the letterform latitude made possible through photographically generated typography.[13]

However, within these narrow design guidelines there was considerable regional and individual variety in the artwork. Some cities, villages, and communes were famous for their imagery. The port city of Luda (now Dalian, in Liaoning Province) has a historical tradition of woodcut printmaking, which blossomed during the GPCR. Peasant-style paintings from Huxian County (Shaanxi Province) became a local industry after the County Communist Party Committee organized art classes.

The following are examples of the various stylistic features and genres evident in the collection.

1. Hand-printed woodcut

2. Woodcut illustration, large-edition offset reproduction

3. Bold, graphically driven imagery

4. Classical watercolor landscape painting style

5. Huxian peasant paintings

6. Watercolor paintings with graphic outlines

7. Large poster composed of two or more segments

8. Oil painting

Posters produced after the GPCR began to display a broader diversity of styles, reflecting the deep changes in political authority and policies. Abstraction resurfaced, as did photographic and photorealistic treatments of natural landscapes and classical-style illustrations.

A. Abstraction

B. Undeveloped natural landscape

C. Classical imagery and style

---

12 Andrews, 359.

13 Robbin Henderson, production manager for the San Francisco China Books art department, 1986–1991. Interview by Lincoln Cushing, August 2006.

Many of these posters utilize visual shorthand to indicate key concepts. Major examples include:

1. **Model operas.** Of the thirteen or so revolutionary operas (essentially dramatic ballets with song), eight of the most popular were termed "The Eight Model Works" and were a significant cultural presence during the GPCR. The example shown is from *The Story of the Red Lantern*.

2. **The Paris Commune.** The radical government that controlled Paris during the spring of 1871, although it ultimately failed, was deemed by Karl Marx a significant model for proletarian revolution.

3. **Red ribbon flowers.** These traditional symbols of success are seen in posters celebrating and honoring successful worker-students.

4. **Yanan.** Mao and the Red Army camped here from 1937 to 1947, after the Long March strategic retreat from the Guomindang (Kuomintang). It was during Mao's stay in Yanan that he deepened his analysis of the factors that would lead to the success of the Chinese Communist Party. Several features represent this locale, including cave dwellings and the pagoda shown here, one of the only buildings to survive Japanese bombing.

5. **Foreigners.** Non-Chinese were represented by stereotypical dress (e.g., sombreros and serapes for Latin Americans, dashikis for Africans) and physical features.

6. **Red armbands.** Originally worn by the militia, these were adopted by the Red Guards, students, and others intending to show their loyalty to Mao Zedong's line during the early period of the GPCR.

7. **"Workers, peasants, and soldiers."** Long-undervalued social groups were the backbone of revolutionary legitimacy during the GPCR. This peasant has the additional iconographic quality of representing a national minority, usually indicated by slightly different facial features and national dress.

8. **Ordinary citizen role models.** Everyday people rose to national stature through extraordinary hard work and heroism. Lei Feng was a soldier in the People's Liberation Army.

9. **Norman Bethune.** This Canadian doctor lent his skills to the Chinese during their resistance to Japanese occupation in the late 1930s. His service and death while assisting the Chinese communists made him one of the few Western national heroes in China, especially during the GPCR. This image also shows another icon, pine tree branches, which sometimes represent personal discipline, wisdom, and endurance.

10. **Mao's most famous books.** Although Mao wrote numerous political documents, these books were published in the millions and represented his thoughts in print: *Quotations from Chairman Mao Tse-tung*, published in 1964, and *Selected Works of Mao Tse-tung*, published in 1966.

11. **Red.** In general the color represents socialism and revolution, and the red sun symbolized Mao as well as "Mao Zedong Thought." Images of Mao himself also symbolized the revolution and Marxism–Leninism–Mao Zedong Thought.

12. **Other visual media.** Supplemental text and images appear within posters as a way to reinforce the subject. This is most obvious in outdoor images that include the text of giant banners, but many posters with interior scenes—such as schools, private homes, libraries, political meetings, and political offices—also incorporate reproductions of other Chinese posters.

Socialist Realist Icons

Because of their artistic orthodoxy, codified imagery, and energized political tone, these posters became emblematic of the GPCR. Their iconographic style later served as a rich source for artistic and political interpretation, ranging from exploitative derivatives to clever homages. In everything from rock posters to commercial advertising, "Chinese poster style" was a recognized symbol of active revolution.

Shortly before U.S. President Richard Nixon traveled to China in 1973, opening up new diplomatic channels between the two countries, Andy Warhol produced a series of silkscreen paintings of Mao Zedong, based on Zhang Zhenshi's official portraits.

Mr. Zhang's series of images (the first of which was painted in 1950 and was slightly modified over time) hung in Tiananmen Square and were often reproduced as poster art.

The 1978 catalog cover for a British alternative book distributor was a particularly well-done example of parody. The front cover shows a crowd of energetic militants moving as one, but as the image continues seamlessly to the back cover, the people jam into a wall—a critique of the perils of uncritical mass thought. Another poster from the same year by San Francisco Bay Area artist Pat Ryan illustrates how the genre was fodder for media in the U.S. counter-culture community by appropriating classic GPCR imagery and icons and transforming it to reflect local issues.

A more recent example comes from U.S. cartoonist Kirk Anderson, who uses the vernacular of GPCR posters as "totalitarian art" to comment on George W. Bush's government policies.

Chinese Poster Resonance with Movement Communities

The Chinese revolution and its visual depiction in posters inspired many people around the world, for a variety of reasons. Without even knowing the details of Chinese events, viewers could appreciate

Concrete Foundation of the Arts, Pat Ryan, 1978. 57 x 71 cm.

Cover from *News from Neasden*, England, 1978, artwork by Clifford Harper.

Web cartoon by Kirk Anderson, 2006.

some of these posters as rare positive depictions of disenfranchised communities building a new society. From the students making posters during the May 1968 Paris uprising to the Black Panthers in the United States, groups outside of China paid close attention to the GPCR and its artistic output. These posters served as influential cultural tokens during the 1960s and '70s, reinforcing the revolutionary spirit of numerous communities struggling for self-identification and social change.

Although many organizations were engaged in direct support of China's revolutionary politics, two were instrumental in bringing the posters to a North American audience: China Books and Periodicals and the U.S.–China People's Friendship Association (USCPFA).

China Books, founded in 1960 by a novelist and poet born in China to missionary parents, reached a wide audience through its storefronts in New York, San Francisco, and Chicago and via its mail-order business. For many U.S. scholars and others interested in studying China it was the only practical resource for these materials. Its mail-order catalog from the early 1970s featured nine large-format posters selling for 1 dollar apiece and thirty-four smaller prints at 50 cents each, in subject areas such as "Chinese People," "Mao Tse-tung and Lu Hsun," and "Landscapes." They were sold directly to individuals, but also wholesaled to numerous political bookstores around the country. Nancy Ippolito, who started working at the Chicago branch of China Books in 1978, remembers:

> China Books imported books and other publications directly from the Foreign Language Publishing Bureau, which was set up after the [1949] revolution and was responsible for spreading propaganda to the rest of the world. They usually made their own determination about the quantities of what they sent us—a lot of times it was based on how they sold in China, and given the population difference sometimes it would be disastrous. They sent us posters—thousands and thousands of them, I can't imagine how many. We had a five-story building in downtown Chicago, and when we moved we had to give them away, throw them away. Then about ten years later people would come looking for them, as they became collector's items.
>
> We carried books in all languages too—we had whole floors of the building devoted to Arabic and Farsi, because people actually bought the books in those languages then. We did wholesale sales to bookstores and organizations. The Black Panthers bought huge numbers of things from us, as did the USCPFA and the Revolutionary Communist Party. Also, at different times we'd sell hundreds of these posters for people hosting conferences and the like. We'd sometimes just give them to groups who were doing speaking engagements, as part of our solidarity efforts.
>
> In addition to radicals in this country, these posters appealed to Chinese Americans out of nationalist interest, who wanted some connection with China and were thrilled to be able to find these things. At the time, many Chinese-Americans who were working towards normalizing relations between the U.S. and China did not want to go to the Chinatown stores, which were mostly very reactionary.[14]

The USCPFA began in the San Francisco Bay Area in 1972 and two years later became a national organization building people-to-people diplomacy between the United States and China. They hosted film screenings, concerts, forums, exhibits, and other events at which posters were sold.

14 Nancy Ippolito. Interview by Lincoln Cushing, August 2006.

In 1967, before the founding of the Revolutionary Communist Party U.S.A. (RCP), which claims to continue to uphold the spirit of Mao's revolution, RCP leader Bob Avakian saw a Mao poster on the apartment wall of Eldridge Cleaver, a Black Panther and militant role model. When Bob asked Eldridge why he displayed that poster, he was told: "We've got that picture of Mao Tse-tung up on the wall because Mao Tse-tung is the baddest motherf***er on the planet Earth!"[15] The RCP and other self-described Maoist organizations were later instrumental in dissemination of the Chinese posters within the United States.

African Americans

An online exhibit of posters from the Chinese Cultural Revolution mounted by CNN.com includes a 1971 image titled "Long Live Marxism, Leninism, and Mao Zedong Thought!" [see page 101, middle left], with this provocative caption:

> The slogans on the left and on the right say: "Proletariat of the World, Unite!" Represented are fighters from the Middle East, Africa, and Asia with the Chinese man in the center. This iconography shows the essence of revolution; did the Black Panthers learn from such imagery?[16]

In fact, there was significant political exchange between the Chinese communist government and African Americans in the United States. In a 2001 interview, Black Panther Party member Jamal Joseph said:

> The connection between the Black Panther party and Cuba and Vietnam and China and North Korea and many liberation movements throughout the world was that we saw the struggle for liberation as a global struggle, and people were talking about the same issues: These issues came down to human rights, anti-war, anti-racism, economic empowerment, but usually we talked about class struggle. And you

really saw that the struggle didn't come down to black or white or red or brown, but to the haves and the have-nots.[17]

U.S. Black Power activist Robert F. Williams, author of *Negroes with Guns,* went into political exile in 1961, living in various socialist countries and ending up in China from 1966 to 1969. Williams published a major article on Black Power in the August 1966 issue of *Peking Review,* two months before the official founding of the Black Panther Party for Self Defense (later simply the Black Panther Party, or BPP). It is widely acknowledged that the Black Panther Party's public posture of armed resistance was deeply influenced by Williams's vision, and the Panthers' view of the Party as the vanguard of the revolution, working to establish a united front, paralleled Maoist ideology. In 1968, the BPP began selling copies of the Little Red Book to raise funds. In 1970, a broad grouping of U.S. activists visited North

Kathleen Cleaver at the San Francisco Black Panther Party office, 1968. Photograph by Copeland, the *Berkeley Barb,* October 25–31, 1968.

15 Bob Avakian, Chairman of the Central Committee of the Revolutionary Communist Party U.S.A., Cleveland, *Summing Up the Black Panther Party* (excerpt from a speech, 1979). www.rwor.org/a/1212/baback.html.

16 From the Web version of Cable Network News: www.cnn.com/interactive/specials/9908/china.revolution.posters/content/poster12.html.

Korea, North Vietnam, and China as the U.S. People's Anti-Imperialist Delegation, including BPP officers Elaine Brown and Eldridge Cleaver. As a result of that trip, the Chinese government invited a larger delegation of the Black Panther Party to visit in 1971.

Kathleen Cleaver, the communications secretary for the Black Panther Party from 1967 to 1971, remembers the posters distinctly:

> Because China is so far away, we saw very few posters. What was influential was a style, a Chinese style, one that we absorbed from just a few posters. This was opposed to the Cuban posters, where we saw a lot of them. There are students who will say that the BPP was a Maoist organization, which is not true. But the reason they say that is that we read the Red Book, we had rules of discipline that came out of the Red Book, and many of our newspaper covers had a Chinese style. [Party cofounder] Huey Newton complained to one of the editors [Raymond Lewis], "Raymond, our paper is for people in America, not in the PRC." It's a distinct style.
>
> There was one Chinese poster in particular, which I had up on my wall in the SNCC [Student Nonviolent Coordinating Committee] office, that I used as a cover for a Black Liberation reader for students and activists following a conference that we held in 1967. The reason this poster is significant is that there are three figures on the poster, very stylized, with arrows and guns, and one of them is black. By 1967 there was a sense that Chinese art was reaching out to the African liberation movement and to the Black liberation movement, at the same time that we were getting in touch with their art.
>
> The posters that we are talking about are very specifically Chinese communist ones from dur-ing the GPCR, a very precise slice of Chinese posters that corresponded to the highest period of influence of the Red Book in this country. We were responding to Lin Biao's notion of a people's war. During the GPCR few activists and revolutionaries in the U.S. had a really clear appreciation of Chinese history—they read things that Mao wrote, and they read things written about Mao. But it was . . . the GPCR, and the posters, along with other things coming out of China at the time, that were part of the "vibe." They were ubiquitous. They symbolized the height of revolution. That's enough. We didn't have all the details. We'll never get all the details.[18]

Asian Americans

Activism in the Asian American community in the United States happened to run very high all during the GPCR period. Rooted in the economic and racial inequalities of San Francisco's Chinatown, the Red Guard Party (RGP) was one of many groups that sought to educate, agitate, and organize among communities of color all around the United States. On March 22, 1969, the RGP unveiled its "Ten-Point Program." This document was modeled on a similar one developed earlier by the Black Panther Party, an organization with which the RGP had close contact. The I Wor Kuen (Society of the Fist of Harmony—an allusion to the Chinese anti-imperialist Boxer Rebellion fighters in the early 1900s) emerged the same year in New York, and the two groups merged in 1971. Numerous other community-based organizations sprang up in the following years. Although there was a great amount of local design talent that created its own imagery for these groups, the poster iconography of China was nonetheless very influential.

17 Jamal Joseph. Interview by Jonathan Fischer, summer 2001. www.docspopuli.org/articles/Trikont.html.

18 Kathleen Cleaver. Interview by Lincoln Cushing, August 2006.

Steve Louie, a third-generation Chinese American and social movements scholar and author, described the impact of China and its posters on United States activism:

My introduction to the Little Red Book and to Mao—and actually the whole idea of China as a political entity—came about because of the Black Panthers, because of my interest in the Civil Rights and Black Power movements. In the same sort of sense, the China posters were an influence—I had an opportunity to travel around the United States in 1970 to 1972, touching base with a lot of people in the Asian American movement in half a dozen major cities, and the China posters were pretty ubiquitous. There were many reasons why people liked them. One was that they showed a country, a Third World country, that had become very strong, and that was standing up to U.S. imperialism, especially around the Vietnam war. The Socialist Realism style was powerful, even though people today look at that and think it looks kind of hokey—it's conventional wisdom among people that that style was over-the-top, but in the context of the seventies it really wasn't, it was actually pretty cool. [Second], when you started looking at posters like the long one with Asian, African, white, and Latino people [see page 107 middle] you saw the strong character of the people, and their determination, that was really inspiring to minorities in this country. That really did

The Asian Community Center office
in San Francisco.
Photograph by Steve Louie, 1968.

resonate a lot with people—I saw that poster *everywhere*. I saw that in the [Young] Lords office, I saw that in Black Panther offices, I saw that in Asian organization offices, I saw that in so many different places.

The third way was kind of like a different political current, perhaps, but the China posters spoke to the possibility of a different kind of society, one where people's lives were valued as opposed to profit . . . during the seventies there was a lot of that counterculture, counter-establishment kind of thinking going on at the time. That was really important in terms of why groups like the Association [USCPFA] were so important and so powerful. I was in the Association in San Francisco for quite a number of years, and through the film showings at the Kabuki, the Friendship Association events that took place, a lot of people—everyday Americans of every nationality, but mostly white at the time—were really attracted to the idea that there was an alternative, and the posters spoke to that. And these were different kinds of posters, not just the "faces in profile" one—they were the posters that showed women telephone linesmen, and commune scenes, and others. The slogan "Women hold up half the sky" was a big deal in the Association, people would talk to that in all sorts of different ways, and you didn't have to be a radical to get behind all of that.[19]

This photograph (facing page) from the Asian Community Center on San Francisco's Kearny Street shows some of the Chinese posters on the walls. The ACC was a multipurpose community and social services center that housed programs for youth on the weekends, drop-in services for older men during the day, and a monthly food distribution program.

Women

The influence of the Chinese posters extended beyond the struggles for ethnic and racial equality to embrace the emerging women's movement. Cathy Cade's 1973 photograph "Gail and Kate Rebuild My VW Engine" shows two women performing the sort of task that broke gender stereotypes. Featured prominently on the wall of their workshop is a copy of "Strive to speed up the mechanization of agriculture," 1971 [see page 73 top]. Kate Kauffman, one of the women in the photograph, described the context:

> I took a class for women at Breakaway: A Women's Liberation School, which demystified auto mechanics, and then Gail invited me to join her in her backyard garage. I was so excited to be using my body and tools. Raised as an upper-middle-class girl, this had been off-limits to me. Nontraditional work was highly regarded in the lesbian community. I got a lot of positive reinforcement from my peers.

She also commented on the role of the Chinese posters:

> We were excited about images of nontraditional women, which were rare. And we were delighted

19 Steve Louie. Interview by Lincoln Cushing, July 2006.

"Gail and Kate Rebuild My VW Engine."
Photograph by Cathy Cade, 1973.

about the apparently positive "Women Hold Up Half the Sky" campaign that was going on in China at the time. The fact that the posters were Communist propaganda was a plus at that moment in time, as we then identified as anti-imperialist feminist socialists.[20]

Exhibitions and Scholarship

Although formal study of the GPCR within China is generally limited to emphasizing its excesses and supporting the current regime's position, there is a growing amount of broader scholarship taking place outside China.

During the GPCR there was virtually no formal contact between China and the United States. Only as relations between the two normalized in 1979 were exhibits of this period's cultural products shared with the world. One of the earliest was "Peasant Paintings from Huhsien [Huxian]," mounted at the Otis Art Institute (currently the Otis Institute of Art and Design) in Los Angeles in 1978. It featured about eighty gouache paintings from the art movement started in Shaanxi Province during the Great Leap Forward in 1958. The reviewer for the *Los Angeles Times* admired the works but could not resist some cynicism about the message: "Chinese propaganda art is infinitely more decorative and palatable than the Soviet version. Instead of being assaulted with nasty attacks on round-eyed Imperialists, we see relentlessly idyllic depictions of Chinese workers toiling for the revolution with glee." Some of these paintings, such as *A Commune Fish Pond*, painted in 1973, had already been produced as posters; this particular one was extremely popular, with two printings totaling more than three million in March of 1973. The review continues: "In 'A Commune Fish Pond' the catch leaps enthusiastically into nets, tickled pink to provide revolutionary sustenance for the workers."[21]

A few poster exhibits appeared soon afterward. Aside from a small 1970 exhibit in Sweden curated by Jon Sigurdson, the first large exhibition was the collection at the University of Westminster (England) shown in London in 1979. A second wave of exhibits started in the mid-1990s from collections both within and outside of China. In 1996, the University of Wisconsin–Madison's Elvehjem Museum of Art (now the Chazen Museum of Art) hosted the exhibit "Mao's Graphic Voice: Pictorial Posters from the Cultural Revolution," a selection from a private collection in Shanghai. In 1999, an exhibit titled "Picturing Power: Posters from the Chinese Cultural Revolution" was shown at Indiana University's East Asian Studies Center. The exhibition then went to Ohio State University and a series of European venues—but, interestingly, was not shown in any major U.S. city. "Picturing Power" was drawn entirely from the 1979 University of Westminster collection, and both institutions collaborated in producing the book *Picturing Power in the People's Republic of China*. This exhibit and book represented a significant step in promoting these materials as tools for broader China scholarship. As noted in the exhibit's introductory essay,

> One sees in these posters many things revealed about patterns of social organization which suggest that, even during the upheavals of the Cultural Revolution, not everything changed by any means. The way men as opposed to women figure in the posters, the way members of particular generational or occupational groups are portrayed, the way economic and social life is envisioned—these all reveal not only ruptures but also continuities. Best of all, at least when it comes to teaching various kinds of publics (of all ages) about China, the posters provide an unusually "student-friendly" medium through which to make points about change and persistence over time.[22]

20 Kate Kauffman. Interview by Cathy Cade, 2006.
21 William Wilson, "A fascinating glimpse of China," *Los Angeles Times Home* magazine, June 18, 1978.

Scholars working with the Hsiao Min Wang Chinese Poster Art Collection at the Claremont Graduate University in California have developed a fresh, interdisciplinary approach to research. Professor John Regan saw the potential of this collection to expand scholarship on the GPCR and started the "Recollections Project" in 1999. The posters were used as a springboard to conduct interviews with ordinary Chinese people about their experiences during the GPCR and the role the posters played in their lives. Here is one of the statements, referring to a poster of Mao with peasants in a cotton field:

> This poster reminded me of the days when I had just graduated from high school in the early seventies. I was one of the four high school graduates of a "Production Brigade." I felt so proud. That's why I was chosen by the Brigade to be the head of women and head of the experiment group for cotton growing. The villagers regarded me as an educated person. Almost every day we worked until 10 at night. I took with me some steamed bread from my home. Though my mother was very supportive [she] still felt that I was a little crazy because food was not plentiful at that time. Finally our group succeeded in the experiment. The cotton grew tall and bore larger flowers. I became the model cotton grower and was asked to attend the meeting of experience exchange. I stayed at the municipal guesthouse; it was the first time that I slept on a spring bed. Before that I had only heard of such a bed. Other model laborers and I were conferred big red paper flowers on the chest [see page 85 top], and we marched in the front of the parade all the way to the meeting place in the stadium. At the meeting, I was so excited to see the national model farmer who went to Beijing and met Mao. Our group was therefore named after this model. Then I was advised to join the Party, for

us a great sign of respect. But I did not think so. I was a woman and should not be so ambitious and also I was well over the age to marry. My villagers already called me an "old girl." I was married much later than others. That period is always a beautiful remembrance.[23]

Numerous shows appeared in the early 2000s, including "Art of the Great Proletarian Cultural Revolution," which toured three Canadian cities during 2002–2003 and produced some new works designed to enhance understanding of the culture during this period. Dr. Stefan R. Landsberger, a Sinologist at Leiden University and professor at the University of Amsterdam in the Netherlands, has assembled one of the largest known collections of these posters. His archive is now housed at the International Institute of Social History in Amsterdam. Among Dr. Landsberger's many contributions is his compilation of detailed biographical data on the individual artists.

Finally, the posters in this book all come from a larger body of work that has been donated as the "Ann Tompkins *(Tang Fandi)* and Lincoln Cushing Chinese Poster Collection" to the East Asian Library of the University of California, with a smaller set of duplicate copies going to the Center for the Study of Political Graphics in Los Angeles. It is hoped that they will become part of the renewed scholarship in studies of political poster art and the Great Proletarian Cultural Revolution.

22 Stephanie Donald, Harriet Evans, and Jeffery Wasserstrom, "Chinese Political Posters as Social and Historical Documents." Essay from the 1999 exhibit "Picturing Power: Posters from the Chinese Cultural Revolution." www.indiana.edu/~easc/exhibit/project.html.

23 Interview with oral history subject "female peasant, age 45 or above, in a small town in Northwest China." www.cgu.edu/pages/3052.asp.

People, Poverty, Politics, and Posters by Ann Tompkins

When I lived in China, the bookstores in the heart of downtown Beijing were wonderful places to explore. One, on Wangfujing Street, offered shelves of new books in Chinese and great expanses of tables holding secondhand books, including a section of foreign titles, which interested me because I couldn't read Chinese. In another, on the first floor I saw only Chinese-language books. I climbed up the stairs to the second floor, which seemed to be mainly maps and technical materials. Climbing to the third floor, I was rewarded by a great array of colorful posters. Here was art that spoke to my heart. What's more, since they were 3 to 33 fen each (then about 1 to 11 cents U.S.), it was the first time that I could afford to buy all the art my heart desired. *I'll take this one, and that one.* I impulsively rattled off identifying numbers attached to the corners of the posters hung all around the room. After I had ordered a big batch, the bookstore worker gathered them, rolled them up, and neatly tied them with string. He then wrapped the long roll in a narrow strip of brown paper—not more than four inches wide—which he deftly tucked in at one end, rolled diagonally, and tucked in at the other end, conserving paper that was generally scarce. It was the end of 1965, and I was just beginning to learn about China and the ways of the Chinese people.

I had seen one or two of these posters before, on the walls in offices of various neighborhood committees and work sites I had visited during my first two-week tour of China in late November or early December 1965. I would see more over the next four years on billboards as I rode my bicycle along the main streets of Beijing (such as the poster at the top of page 101), in stores and clinics, and in the homes of peasants whom I came to know as friends. Over the years in Beijing and in later travels around China, I took every opportunity to check out bookstores to see if I could add to my treasure stash. Initially, I chose posters

based on my taste in the art and for their political content. I was moved by the cheerful portrayal of workers and peasants as important figures, images of women in new roles, and pictures that called for solidarity among the peoples of all countries. Later I selected posters that reminded me of events and places, issues, and politics that had come to have meaning for me and would serve as memories of my time in China. Prior to being there, I knew very little of Chinese history or culture other than having a general awareness of its struggles against Japanese invasion and of the country's civil war between the forces led by the Communist Party [*Gongchangdang*] and the Nationalist Party [*Guomindang*]. Some posters I bought to remind me of little things, like paper windows and the cut-paper silhouettes used to decorate them, the hard platforms called *kangs* where the whole family slept in peasant homes, and shoes sewn by hand (including the soles) [see page 115 top]. Others recall major events such as the Red

Office of a neighborhood committee in China. Photograph by Ann Tompkins, date unknown.

Guard movement and issues of various campaigns in the Great Proletarian Cultural Revolution [see pages 118 and 125]. Ultimately I began to select posters to show changes I noticed over time in the content and style. These selections were less circumscribed by my personal taste, but by 1996 were somewhat limited due to the dwindling number of posters from which to choose. Despite my persistence in collecting, I never intended to amass a collection representative or definitive of the full range of Chinese revolutionary posters.

My interest in going to China had primarily grown out of my experience as a social worker in the United States. It seemed that the problem of hunger and other social ills grew faster than we as social workers could do anything about them. Having grown up to the urging that I should eat all of my food and "remember, there are hungry and starving children in China," now I sought to learn whether China, unlike the United States, had actually found a way to feed and meet the basic needs of its large population.

My family background also helped lead me to China. My parents owned and lived on an 85-foot schooner named *Wander Bird,* which they operated rather like a sailing summer camp. My mother chose

Poster over doorway to the home of peasant friends from Evergreen Commune, Beijing, with Ann's roommate Liu Jiarong and a foreign expert from France. Photograph by Ann Tompkins, date unknown.

to have her first child in a hospital on terra firma, however, so I was born in Chicago in June 1930, when our oceangoing home was far out at sea in the Atlantic. Over the years, my mother and father had to turn away many young people who wanted to sail with us but had no funds to pay their way. Consequently, my parents' interest was aroused when, in the early 1930s, they happened to meet a Soviet sailing ship in the Baltic that was carrying people from various walks of life who had chosen a sailing vacation, with all expenses paid by the Soviet government. After my parents discussed trying to arrange a similar sponsorship by the U.S. government, only to have the idea firmly rebuffed as "communism" by the Morgans and Duponts who had happily sent their sons to sea on our ship, my parents eventually began serious inquiry into communism and things Soviet. Much reading and many lively political discussions ensued in what we called the after cabin (our living quarters). Though such talk was generally above my head when I was ten and eleven, I nevertheless found it very interesting. Against the background of daily news about World War II, the atrocities of concentration camps and fascist rule, I began my own lifelong interest in understanding why wars happen, why a Hitler exists, why racism exists, and why there are so many poor and hungry people.

My first memory about anything Chinese other than hungry children was when, in my early teen years, I heard the great African American singer Paul Robeson sing *The Internationale* not only in English but also in Chinese. In 1949, when I was nineteen, I recall hearing an astounding presentation of the news one day. The radio reporter, without a trace of humor or sarcasm, announced that the armies of Chiang Kai-shek were in Taiwan and had the Communists "all bottled up on the mainland." In fact, the Communist-led People's Army had taken mainland China, and Chiang and his Nationalist Party government had retreated to the island of Taiwan. So it was that I learned of the victory of the Chinese people in their civil war.

In the middle of my senior year at college, while working for a degree in elementary education, I was asked to sign a "loyalty oath" required by the State of California for those in the teaching profession. I refused to go along with what I considered (and the U.S. Supreme Court many years later affirmed) was an infringement of my right to freedom of thought, expression, and association. A switch to an undergraduate major in social work preserved most of my credits and offered hope of private employment without any so-called loyalty oaths. After earning a master's degree in social work, with a specialty in group work, at the University of California at Berkeley, I held jobs in New York and San Francisco in various settings with good and caring social-worker colleagues. But one by one, they all sought higher degrees and administrative positions because they needed incomes to support families, although it was clear that our field was not solving the problems of hunger and poverty. Disappointed by both the social-work field and my colleagues, in 1965 I accepted a friend's suggestion and decided to attend the World Peace Congress being held that summer in Helsinki. I was seeking solutions to poverty and injustice.

The Peace Congress was an amazing event with people from many countries and the largest-ever delegation from the United States (some ninety people, as I recall). There was also a sizable Chinese delegation—offering a rare opportunity for those of us from the United States to speak directly with Chinese people at a time when there were no diplomatic relations between the two countries—so I initiated a meeting between U.S. and Chinese delegates. I also struggled for what seemed to be simple democratic process—the rights of individuals and delegations to speak both within the U.S. delegation's meetings and in the plenary session meetings of the entire Congress. Little did I understand the impact of the things I did and said. There had been a behind-the-scenes effort to prevent the Chinese delegation from being allowed to speak on the plenary floor. When I tried to distribute our statement supporting the Chinese delegation's right to speak, I found that all of the photocopiers were suddenly "not working," was told the key to a room I needed access to was "lost," and encountered other suspicious impediments to using facilities said to be available to all Peace Congress participants. (A British delegate and supporter finally paid to have copies made outside the congress.) Within the U.S. delegation, meetings were suddenly moved with selective notice given to some delegates, and the delegation co-chairs conspicuously avoided calling on me to speak—actions so flagrant that other delegates objected, informing me of new meeting locations and ultimately forcing the co-chairs to give me the floor. At the end of the conference the Chinese delegation asked me if I would like to visit China. I certainly wanted to, but with the provision that I would like to work there awhile, since I would not be able to absorb much in a visit of a few weeks. I waited in London until the official invitation came from Beijing. Both my hosts and I ignored the fact that my passport said I could not travel to communist countries. It was the U.S. government, not China, that prevented U.S. citizens from traveling to the People's Republic of China and other "communist-controlled countries," a policy the U.S. Supreme Court eventually ruled unconstitutional in Aptheker vs. U.S. State Department. When I arrived in Beijing in November 1965, China had diplomatic relations with 50 countries (it hardly seemed "isolated"). I was treated to a two-week tour of important places in China as a guest of the Chinese Peace Committee before I accepted an offer to work as a teacher of college-level English at the Beijing Language Institute *(Beijing Yuyan Xueyuan).*

As a teacher from abroad, I was working under a department named the Foreign Experts Bureau and thus, with no other qualification, was deemed a "foreign expert." I was given a room in the Friendship Hotel, which was actually a very large walled compound that had a guard at the entrance, many large multistory buildings, roadways, garden areas, theaters, stores, and five large dining rooms. The living style was very fancy by Chinese standards, with steam heat and hot running water in every room, window curtains, bedspreads, and plush rugs, as well as a large staff and a fleet of cars at one's service. I lived there for almost a year (from mid-November 1965 to October 1966), and began to learn about China, the Chinese language, and the unfolding Great Proletarian Cultural Revolution. My workplace was less than a half-mile away, and a chauffeured car was provided daily for transportation. I was busy designing lesson plans and learning my students' names, which were hard for me to remember.

The Chinese translation of my surname required five characters, too many for me to learn to write and awkwardly excessive compared to the usual three, or even two, for Chinese names. To simplify, I chose the Chinese character *tang* [汤] (meaning "soup," which has water in it) for the initial sound in Tompkins and as a nod to our seafaring life, followed by the characters *fan* [反] and *di* [帝], which were meaningful both as a word and as a pun on sounds. Ann Tompkins, or "Ann T.," sounds like "anti," and *fandi* means anti-imperialist. So Tang Fandi—or, one might say, Anti-Imperialist Soup—became my Chinese name. My students jumped to their feet as I entered the classroom (the thunderous noise startled me the first few times), greeted me as Teacher Tang Fandi, paid close attention in class, and worked hard to prepare their lessons and memorize overnight vocabulary lists of twenty-five words or more. They were bemused by the faces I made as I struggled with their pronunciation problems, and when I became a little more secure as a teacher we had

fun as openhearted people getting acquainted with each other's ways.

It was in May 1966 that I first noticed signs of the major events unfolding: my students began coming to classes unprepared, falling asleep at their desks, or missing class altogether—all previously unheard-of behaviors. As fewer students came to class and activities of the growing Cultural Revolution increasingly consumed their time and attention, Institute leaders announced that regular classes were called off for the summer. The students all continued living at the college and were very busy in the activities of the Cultural Revolution. They remained in the Institute until some three years later, when they were finally given work assignments as part of the ongoing phases of the revolution. I experienced this beginning in my institute, but it was happening all over Beijing, and to my understanding was rapidly developing in a similar way in other large and medium-size cities across China. Though classes were called off for the summer, in fact it turned out to be years before most regular classes were resumed on a full-time basis in high schools, colleges, and universities throughout China.

That summer of 1966 I was among a group of perhaps twenty-five or thirty foreign teachers taken on a three-week trip to various cities and historic locations of China. While I appreciated this very much, it felt as though no one at either the Foreign Experts Bureau or our Institute knew quite what to do with us. On this trip, we saw that there were special discussion activities going on in many places, as at an enamel factory in the city of Xian (Sian) where the big-character posters, or *dazibao*, were already evident in abundance.

August brought publication of a key document, "Decision of the Central Committee of the Chinese Communist Party Concerning the Great Proletarian Cultural Revolution," providing guidelines for conducting the revolution. From this document, which was informally called "The Sixteen Points," I learned of a socialist education movement already taking place in the countryside, that the Cultural Revolution would be conducted in close conjunction with it, and that "cultural and educational units and leading organs of the Party and Government in large and medium cities are the points of concentration of the present Proletarian Cultural Revolution."

While it was a busy and exciting time for the Chinese people, without work (though paid regularly as I was throughout my stay) I turned to studying Chinese in the language classes that continued to be held for foreign students at our institute. In keeping with the movement, as the semester progressed our texts were being rewritten to emphasize studying quotations from Chairman Mao, without any basic progression of vocabulary acquisition. Nevertheless, I was learning some Chinese and vocabulary that was very useful for participating in the Great Proletarian Cultural Revolution.

There was sharp debate among the foreigners living in the Friendship Hotel, as well as those who had lived in their work units as longtime resident workers, about whether participation in the Cultural Revolution was just for the Chinese. I took part in political study groups with other English-speaking foreigners while trying to keep abreast of the rapidly changing events. Most of my foreign friends had firsthand experience of many previous mass campaigns in China that had mobilized millions of people, including one aimed at eradicating prostitution, and another pitting the people against flies. They spoke enthusiastically about the mobilization to make iron in localized furnaces during the Great Leap Forward, about government policies that saved many lives during the famine years, and about the use of criticism and self-criticism in campaigns to define the direction of the Party and improve its work. Massive educational campaigns were not new to China and, in their view, had been productive despite various acknowledged shortcomings.

My closest friends, my comrades, were Sid Engst and Joan Hinton. In 1946 and 1948 they had come to China separately, each crossing through the firing lines of the war front from the Nationalist Government–held area to Communist–held areas. They were married in Yanan and had lived, worked, and raised three children among the peasants in rural China. They were fluent in Chinese and had participated in many previous mass mobilizations. Another close friend, Bertha Sneck, also a longtime resident and worker in China, lived in the Foreign Languages Press compound and often accompanied me to work with the peasants at Evergreen Commune. I found myself in agreement with these people. We believed that participation in the GPCR was a matter of one's class stand, an issue of whether you side with the working people or the exploiters and oppressors. On this basis, and after a week of intense discussion, the four of us took a chance and wrote our own *dazibao* taking on the Foreign Experts Bureau. We wanted to know, and titled our *dazibao*, "Why Is It That Foreigners Working Here at the Heart of the World Revolution Are

Big-character posters *(dazibao)* in an enamel factory, Xian, P.R.C. Photograph by Ann Tompkins, summer 1966.

Being Pushed Down the Revisionist Road?" The next line asked, "What monsters are behind the treatment of foreigners working in China?" We detailed the treatment we objected to and ended with seven requests, including that we be treated not like bourgeois experts but like class brothers, that we be permitted and encouraged to join physical labor, and that our living standard be the same as that of the Chinese personnel of the same category.

Out of our own respect for Chinese sovereignty, we mailed a copy of our poster to the Cultural Revolution Central Group at the main Party headquarters rather than simply putting it up on a wall, as the Chinese around us were doing. Then, without mentioning that we had mailed one anywhere, we gave a copy to the main office of the Foreign Experts Bureau. Afterward, we returned to wandering Beijing's downtown streets, reading the newest crop of posters plastered everywhere, including an amusing one protesting that it was wrong for traffic lights in a socialist country to use red for "stop" and green for "go." Anybody wrote whatever they chose to say, addressing major or minor issues. In the ferment of ideas, creativity was contagious. Shortly thereafter, we heard that our poster was pasted up on a wall in the lobby of the Foreign Languages Press. We ran to see. I couldn't read the whole poster, but could recognize my signature. All around our *dazibao* were others supporting our position, which had been posted by foreigners from several countries. (I do not recall hearing of any that opposed ours at that time, but it is likely that some did.) Very soon after, I was taken to an invitational gathering hosted by one of the most famous of Chinese revolutionaries, Chen Yi. He informed us and the supporters of our position that Chairman Mao had read our *dazibao*, which became known as "The Four American *Dazibao*," and had written a note on September 8 supporting the position and demands in our *dazibao*. We were elated!

As a consequence of that September 8 instruction (*jiu ba pishi*), I was able to promptly move out of the hotel and into the Institute, where I was greeted with a gift of the *Quotations from Chairman Mao Tsetung* in Chinese; assigned to share a room with Liu Jiarong, one of my former students; and welcomed to take part in the Cultural Revolution discussion meetings and activities of the Institute. I negotiated to lower my salary to that of my co-teachers. It was lowered, but as I did not know the amount the others got, it was a long time before I found out that it was still very high by Chinese standards.

I continued to visit friends at the Friendship Hotel. People from some sixty-five countries quickly joined a new organization that we set up and, in the style of the other groups then forming in work and study units across Beijing, named the Bethune-Yanan Rebel Regiment. The Cultural Revolution at this point was a movement to distinguish right from wrong, to criticize the "Four Olds"—old ideas, old culture, old habits, old customs—and to apply this to the leadership in our relevant work units. Our meetings were conducted in five languages, a lesson in patience, but also a very exciting expression of worldwide unity. In addition to arranging to sit together by language so translations could be heard more easily, we numbered the quotations in our Little Red Books so everyone could be "on the same

Roommates Tang Fandi (Ann Tompkins) and Liu Jiarong in their dorm room at Beijing Language Institute. Photographer unknown, circa 1967.

page" (on the same quotation) despite the different lengths of languages in print. Our common concern was to study politics, understand events, take part in them in suitable ways, and work for changes in nonproletarian policies of the Foreign Experts Bureau. There were still many foreigners, and some among the Chinese in the Bureau, who frowned on foreigners participating.

My daily life with the Chinese people meant that I began eating the same food in the Institute's dining room as my Chinese colleagues, exercising in the daily general assembly to a routine with music over the loudspeakers, going to large and small meetings, discussing recent events, and even studying a few internal documents (limited to specific levels of circulation). I was able to have students and colleagues read *dazibao* in the Institute to me. By this time, at the end of 1966, all the walls of the Institute's buildings had *dazibao* plastered up on them. When those spaces were filled as high as one could reach and still read the text, wires were strung up like clotheslines, and *dazibao*—often many pages long—were hung wherever one could find a space among the fluttering colorful pages. *Dazibao* were posted whenever anyone or any group chose to put one up, about whatever they fancied to write

about: common topics included administration issues in our Institute, Beijing city politics, education policies, and taking on particular leaders at any level of the Party or government. The tissue paper and supplies for creating the *dazibao* were made available free. And of course, once someone put up one, there were bound to be others in support and in opposition. So, day after day, it was interesting and exciting to go read what was newly posted, see who had responded and how, and decide whether and how one wanted to take part. In the Institute's Come to China Department, which conducted our Chinese language classes, I met an American student named Norman Shulman. Together we wrote—and posted in the lobby of our dormitory building—a *dazibao* calling on the department to integrate the foreign students who wanted to share more fully in the ordinary life of China. Existing policy required them to accept various forms of special treatment such as eating in separate dining rooms serving foreign foods. We asked to allow us all to work at physical labor with the peasants from time to time.

Many people eagerly looked for guidance in the daily newspapers, government speeches, reports, and study materials that were widely distributed and posted. Luckily, there were English translations for many items, so I, along with everyone, studied "The Sixteen Points." "The main target of the present movement is those Party persons in power taking the capitalist road," said Point 5. "The aim of the GPCR is to revolutionize people's ideology and as a consequence to achieve greater, faster, better, more economical results in all fields of work," said Point 14. Point 1 declared, "The proletariat must meet head-on every challenge of the bourgeoisie in the ideological field and use new ideas, culture, customs, and habits of the proletariat to change the mental outlook of the whole of society." Here was the complement to criticizing the Four Olds. We were on the cutting edge of history in creating new ways of thinking and

Out-of-town Red Guards reading and copying the Shulman-Tompkins dazibao and responses to it written by students and faculty at Beijing Language Institute. Photograph by Ann Tompkins, circa 1967.

doing. But we still had to figure out for ourselves what the "capitalist road" was, who was taking it, and what the ideas, culture, customs, and habits of the proletariat were, specifically.

From the day I first arrived, our institute loudspeakers provided daily one-hour news broadcasts of events around the world in countries large and small. We heard about new construction projects; new diplomatic relations; medical and technical advances; people's demonstrations and struggles for independence, freedom, and justice; and all sorts of matters of interest to working and farming people, whether in major powers like France and the United States or in nations like Benin, Mauritania, or Tanzania. I came to appreciate the way Chinese life was organized mainly around work. The large Chinese work units, factories, and colleges provided not only a paycheck but also housing, a dining commons, outdoor movies on Saturday nights in hot or cold weather, and car-and-driver service available by reservation for doctor visits or other needs. The communes and state farms were different in the specifics, but also brought benefits through cooperation that were not possible on an individual basis. I experienced my work unit as a center of life with a kind of collective responsibility, support, and activity that relieved me of many responsibilities I was accustomed to handling as an individual.

One of the highlights of my life in the Institute was participating in meetings to *chi ku,* which literally means "eat bitterness." Elderly Chinese came to tell moving stories of their lives in the old society, recalling their poverty and troubles with landlords and bosses. We ate a plain, coarse-grain food that reminded me of the Jewish custom of eating bitter herbs at Passover to recall past tribulations. I attended an exhibition of life-size clay sculptures called "The Rent Collection Courtyard," which vividly depicted how peasants in the old society were cheated by landlords [see pages 91 bottom left and 120 left].

Such experiences were unknown to the Chinese children of the 1960s, who needed this history to be good successors to the revolution. I met older women with tiny bound feet, and understanding the pain and restrictions that the binding process caused, as well as the resultant lifelong limitation of movement, reached me emotionally. This was a practice the 1912 Republic sought to end, but that task was completed in rural areas by the Communist-led revolution.

Among my happiest times in China were my stints of physical labor with the peasant team at the Evergreen Commune (*Sijieqing Gongshe),* where I felt very warmly welcomed and was patiently helped. I felt that we all became friends, despite language limitations. I admired the stamina of the peasants, who worked hard from early to late each day, and was impressed by their practical knowledge and the diligence with which they tried to improve their crops. They spoke frankly and enjoyed a good hearty laugh. I was invited into the peasants' homes, including for a meal that was probably the simplest I've ever eaten, generously shared.

The GPCR unfolded in a series of different phases and initiatives, each presenting various issues and tasks for action; in all cases the decision for how best to implement them was left up to the individual.

Ann and peasant woman friends posing for a picture during a work break at Evergreen Commune, Beijing. Photograph by Bertha Sneck, circa 1967.

Activities included writing *dazibao*, setting up revolutionary administrations in work units and lower government bodies, rethinking Confucianism, and fighting selfish interest, all the while struggling to define key concepts such as bourgeois thinking, revisionism, and proletarian ideals. Although the ultimate aim was to correct problems in the highest levels of the Party itself, in late 1966 and early 1967 I attended some of the early meetings at the local level criticizing leaders of various work units—meetings in which dunce caps were put on people's heads and signs were hung around their necks indicating what the accusations were against them. (See page 121 for an illustration depicting landlords being rebuked in an earlier period.) With my poor understanding of Chinese, I was not able to judge the details of guilt or innocence, or even whether there was persuasive argumentation or refutation. I was uncomfortable about the humiliating use of the signs, caps, and kneeling positions that I saw, and would have been firmly opposed to any physical violence, but felt that overall the exposure of real problems was the paramount issue. In the meetings I attended, the bent positions and the humiliation were the worst treatment that occurred. Some of the criticisms and charges surely had validity, just as surely as some were wrongful in the content of the accusations, the use of humiliation, or both.

In 1966, the trains were made free for travel nationally. In a country where travel was a rare experience for most of the population, millions of young people took the opportunity to travel (most of them wearing homemade or rebel-group locally made red armbands identifying themselves as Red Guards). Initially they flooded into Beijing, eager to see their country's capital, to discuss current events, and to read and copy *dazibao*, which they would later write out again and post in their home communities. And surely they hoped to see Chairman Mao in person. All over Beijing, including in our

Institute, classrooms were cleared of furniture and laid out with straw and bamboo mats where these young people stayed free of charge and spent evening hours studying and discussing their *Quotations from Mao Tse-tung*, the newspapers, and other articles. These inexperienced travelers were also helped with food and clothing (which was especially welcomed by those who had traveled from the warm south to the chilly north). Chairman Mao received them on eight different occasions in Tiananmen Square, where an estimated million Red Guards were present each time. I was in one such large meeting and remember being rather alarmed at the press of people and worried about safety, while at the same time being impressed with their enthusiasm and admiration for Chairman Mao and their socialist society. At one of these mass meetings, the Chairman appeared on the balcony at Tiananmen gate identifying himself as one of them by wearing a green army uniform and a red armband, which thrilled the Red Guard crowd. I had also seen Chairman Mao standing at the rail of the rostrum in Tiananmen Square [see page 111] each year when foreign guests were taken to the reviewing stands immediately below for the huge joyous parades and marvelous firework displays celebrating National

Ann and friend harvesting cabbages at Evergreen Commune after the first freeze. Photograph by Bertha Sneck, circa 1967.

Day, the anniversary of the October 1, 1949, founding of the People's Republic of China. Portraits of Mao Zedong were widespread as my photos on pages 24 and 25 show.

After these waves of Red Guards had gone home, there was a further tide of travel called *da chuan lian* ("establish revolutionary ties by traveling from village to village"), in which students from high schools and colleges took their skills to the countryside, helping with literacy education and technical training, while at the same time learning lessons of perseverance and self-sufficiency from the peasants. When the workers in Shanghai replaced their local city administration by setting up a new one called a Cultural Revolution Group—an action Chairman Mao and others deemed a real proletarian seizure of power—a group of my former students went to Shanghai to learn from the Shanghai model. I was very pleased to be invited to accompany them, but finally decided that I might be too much of a burden with my limited Chinese. Meanwhile, the students who had left Beijing on the free trains were returning from the far corners of China, full of new experiences and amazed at the size and diversity of their country. Some had been to Xinjiang Province, so far west that they met Chinese people who, they said, spoke Chinese and looked like me. Several told me that they had read "The Four American *Dazibao*" in various faraway places.

My experience of the GPCR was that each of the phases of the movement opened people's minds and lives to new ways of thinking and acting. Travel brought new understanding of the vastness and variety of China's land, peoples, and climates; in the process, travelers learned to take care of themselves and to plan ahead, and even developed physically. Taking action on any of the issues afforded practice in making decisions, persuading others, and engaging in self-criticism when wrong. Feudalism was a very long period in Chinese history, and not long past

in 1965. Shaking the ancient grip of rigid ways of thinking was no easy task, but was necessary for the society to go forward. So in the GPCR we found children challenging the feudal style of total obedience to the authority of their parents by now asking the reasons for parental decisions, and some wives also challenged the traditional authority of their husbands. Many women were standing up and taking on new roles. In the city of Wuhan and the surrounding area, I was amazed to see women doing extremely difficult physical tasks such as pulling heavily laden carts [see page 55 top]—often without men, though men were also doing the same work. Not having seen this elsewhere, I wondered whether it was a long-standing treatment of women as beasts of burden, or whether it was a sign of a new equality. The work was hard for both the men and the women, yet the women seemed able to do it. Members of a U.S.–China People's Friendship Association delegation during a 1973 visit to China were given a demonstration of new techniques being used by workers on high-tension electric wires. From watching birds landing on and taking off from power lines, the workers had developed a method of allowing electrical current first to enter and later to pass out of their bodies harmlessly, so that the current could remain on while they did their jobs and power in the area was not disrupted [see page 76]. It was the women of the work group who demonstrated how it was done.

During my stay in China, I read all four volumes of Chairman Mao's *Selected Works* in the English first edition published in Beijing in 1965. I read many other documents and articles found in the *Peking Review,* a weekly published by the Chinese Foreign Languages Press, and the English version of *Hsinhua News,* both distributed worldwide. Among the many things I learned from Chairman Mao's writings was the distinction between *class origin* and *class stand*—one has no control over the class one is born into and shaped by, but does have choice and control over which class one sides with and supports. Additionally I took to heart the policy and work method called "from the masses, to the masses," which held that "the masses are the real heroes," and that "to link oneself with the masses, one must act in accordance with the needs and wishes of the masses. All work done for the masses must start from their needs and not from the desire of any individual, however well-intentioned." Another crucial concept, which I found most Chinese people already understood before the GPCR, was the distinction between the people and the government in countries where exploiting classes remain. Most people I met in China did not hold against me what the U.S. government was doing or had done in China, or its actions in Taiwan, Vietnam, or elsewhere that the Chinese clearly designated "imperialism." [See page 105 bottom.] Several young Red Guard artists presented me with gifts of their original artwork [pages 98 bottom, 99 top left, 110 bottom, and 125 bottom] and a portrait of Liu Hulan, a fierce-eyed young revolutionary who was executed in 1947, at age fifteen, by Nationalist troops—defiant to the end. I was also given posters as gifts by various Red Guards and Red Guard groups in our Institute (and from the opposing sides), often on a holiday such as International Women's Day or Chinese New Year.

On the larger scale of collective GPCR activity, there were many things that I was not personally involved in or could only appreciate at a distance. Chairman Mao's August 5, 1966 *dazibao* at Beijing University, "Bombard the Headquarters," had already invited criticism of the Chinese Communist Party all the way to the top, to uncover and remove "the small number at the top in the Party taking the capitalist road." Of course, I did not have sufficient knowledge about China's politics to understand the specifics of who these people might be. Because Mao did not at first call them out by name, a national debate emerged discussing specific leaders, reviewing their

actions as well as the Marxist principles needed to be able to determine right from wrong.

During 1966 and 1967, I saw (and took part in) the formation of groups in Beijing that would eventually coalesce into two main factions, referred to as the *Tian Pai* (Heaven Side) and the *Di Pai* (Earth Side), which opposed each other, but in fact had no fundamental differences about how best to pursue the goals of the revolution. In our Institute there were, at first, alternating radio broadcasts by rival factions, but later each side would simultaneously blast its own programs over loudspeakers at escalating volume. Offices were suddenly and arbitrarily closed so that workers could engage in political study. Several pernicious theories were advanced and spread through the city like evil winds: one advanced a "bloodlines" theory that attributed to children what might be called the sins of the parents; another spread suspicion of people who had traveled abroad or had relationships with foreigners.

Liu Hulan.
Handmade print by unknown Beijing Language Institute artist. Inscription and text on red gift paper says: "Presented to Tang Fandi. People of the whole world, unite! Destroy U.S. imperialism and all running dogs! Jingang Mountain Revolutionary Rebel Group, March 8, 1967, International Women's Day, Beijing Language Institute." 37 x 26 cm.

As a result of the latter, several people I knew were held incommunicado by factions composed of students and members of the institute where they worked—though they were eventually released unharmed. During these factional struggles, several deaths occurred in fighting between students at institutes across the street from one another on a street where I regularly rode my bicycle. At that time I rode down the street between them, but avoided taking the shortcut through one of them. In one, an iron fence had been torn down and repurposed as spears for both sides. In the other, engineering students developed catapults to hurl bricks at their opposing side. After the deaths, the stunned students held memorials, which were followed by a long period of inactivity at the institutes involved, with many students going home for long periods and the cultural revolution in their organizations becoming "*leng leng qing qing*" (cool cool, cold cold). Factionalism (*paixingzhuyi*), not being able to distinguish between true friends and real enemies, was considered a serious error for revolutionaries.

By early 1969, I saw examples of formalism (*xingshizhuyi*), behavior that emphasized the form of an activity but was empty of revolutionary political content, such as waving the Little Red Book without understanding or applying its contents, wearing Chairman Mao buttons and believing that those who didn't wear them did not love him, or bowing before his portrait with no attempt to make creative applications of his writings—all practices strongly taken to task by the CCP's Ninth Congress in late 1969. Despite this call for correction, even on my departure some six months later, border inspectors cut articles out of my bound English copies of the *Peking Review,* China's internationally distributed news magazine. They also cut photographs that showed only parts of Mao's quotations out of my contact sheets (saying that I might distort the incomplete quotations), and demanded to know why I wrapped my shoes in a newspaper that happened to contain a photo of Chairman Mao.

All of these errors of factionalism and formalism worried and upset me greatly, but I saw them as errors of individuals in a revolution that was being conducted on a massive scale, with millions upon millions of participants who had been encouraged to participate, to study, to speak up, and to act, and were all doing so each in their own way. The errors themselves were proof to me of the very real need, on the one hand, to change people's ideology to new ways of thinking and, on the other hand, to recognize that the Great Proletarian Cultural Revolution overall was a true revolution, not lightly named—an attempt to solve the real problem of which class interests would lead China forward. As Chairman Mao had written:

> A revolution is not a dinner party, or writing an essay, or painting a picture, or doing embroidery; it cannot be so refined, so leisurely and gentle, so temperate, kind, courteous, restrained, and magnanimous. A revolution is an insurrection, an act of violence by which one class overthrows another.[24]

I left China in 1970 because I thought that the Ninth Congress of the CCP had named the various errors and called for their correction and that the Cultural Revolution was coming to an end. I had no idea that

---

24 *The Quotations from Chairman Mao* (English edition, 1966), 11–12.

Silkscreen poster by Richard McNeil announcing Ann's speaking tour engagements, 1971, 39x77 cm. Graphic based on photo of Dazhai commune team.

the following five or six years would be considered part of the Cultural Revolution as well. But I also wanted to get home to participate in all the historic events that were happening there, especially the massive opposition to U.S. participation in the war in Vietnam.

At my homecoming in Sonoma County, California, my mother commented on the contrast between the frightening headlines about the GPCR—daily fare on her radio and in local newspapers—and my regular letters from China, which sounded so normal, describing my daily life, my excitement about the activities I was participating in, and the aims of the GPCR. Naturally, I had not written all the details, as one does not usually scare one's parents, but I had also been truthful and was never in fear myself. Friends urged me to go on a speaking tour, because at that time it was so rare for a U.S. citizen to have lived in China. The first tour I set up in 1970—going south from San Francisco to San Diego and back—was well received by large numbers of just plain curious people as well as political and antiwar activists on and off campuses, and encouraging enough to keep me busy with similar tours for the next several years. Going north in 1973 from San Francisco to Vancouver, Canada, I shared speaking podiums with Jane Uptegrove, another young recent visitor to China. More ambitious were two trips spanning the width of the United States. Two young men joined the first of these, selling books from and about China and sharing the driving. One of them, Richard McNeil, had produced a much admired silkscreen publicity poster for the tour based on a photo of model peasants from Dazhai Commune. Wang Yaohua, who had grown up in China, specialized in Chinese history and culture, and obtained his master's degree in English as a Second Language, shared the speaking and the bookselling on the second national tour and subsequently at the adult evening classes we conducted in several colleges.

Whether on a speaking tour or not, I was also frequently invited to meet with the study sessions of women's consciousness-raising groups, a variety of political organizations, veterans' associations, gay and lesbian collectives, and other groups. They usually already had the *Quotations from Mao Tse-tung*. I demonstrated my ideas on how to use the Little Red Book, making practical applications of its lessons to problems the group presented—my way of turning theory into a practical tool for problem solving. Another application was a series of workshops titled "Criticism/Self-Criticism: A Sign of Love and Concern," which I developed and led in the late 1970s, mainly in Northern California, but also in Oregon and Washington.

Wang Yaohua and I had met while we were helping to found the U.S.–China People's Friendship Association (USCPFA) in San Francisco and married in April 1972. In 1973 we both took part in a three-week USCPFA Delegation visit to China, which for us was followed by a seven-week trip, including a stay as newlyweds in Kaifeng, where Yaohua was present at a first full family reunion since 1946. In 1976 I went to China again with a Women's China Study

Ann speaking about GPCR in United States with poster display backdrop.
Photographer unknown, early 1970s.

36

Group, and in 1979 I served as tour leader for the seventeenth USCPFA Friendship Study Tour. On a short family visit to Kaifeng afterward, we first met our infant adopted son, then living with Fifth Brother's family. With one Chinese parent and one from the United States, and born one month after Deng Xiaoping made a trip to the United States as a step toward normalization of government diplomatic relations, our child was given the grand name Wang Zhongmei, which translates as King of China U.S.A. My husband and I lived with our son in Beijing from 1980 to 1982 and then moved to Dalian. I returned to the United States in fall 1983 with our son, to live with his maternal grandmother. In 1996, our son and I paid a three-week private visit to friends and relatives in Beijing and Dalian, at which time I found few posters and clearly saw the changes in subjects and styles.

After the deaths of both Zhou Enlai and Mao Zedong in 1976, and following the trial of the "Gang of Four," an official evaluation was published in 1981. It was subtitled "Authoritative Assessment of Mao Zedong, the 'Cultural Revolution,' and Achievements of the People's Republic." This 105-page pamphlet,

Wang Yaohua, Ann, and Wang Zhongmei at their first meeting in Kaifeng. Photograph by unidentified family member, 1979.

"Resolution on CPC History (1949–81) in 1981," adopted by the Sixth Plenary Session of the Eleventh Central Committee of the Communist Party of China on June 27, 1981, published in English by the Foreign Languages Press, stated on page 41 (all quotation marks are in the original),

> Chief responsibility for the grave "Left" error of the "cultural revolution," an error comprehensive in magnitude and protracted in duration, does indeed lie with Comrade Mao Zedong.

However, this document also holds, on page 56,

> Comrade Mao Zedong was a great Marxist and a great proletarian revolutionary, strategist, and theorist. It is true that he made gross mistakes during the "cultural revolution," but, if we judge his activities as a whole, his contributions far outweigh his mistakes. His merits are primary and his errors secondary.

In 1982 a long Constitution reflecting new policies replaced the short 1975 Constitution, which had been clearly based on ideas from the Cultural Revolution. Some statues of Mao Zedong were taken down, but some were left, and the portrait at Tiananmen Square remained. In September of 2006, it was announced that Shanghai would introduce newly revised high school history textbooks, which cover socialism in a "single, short chapter in the senior high school history course. Chinese Communism before the economic reform that began in 1979 is covered in a sentence. The text mentions Mao only once—in a chapter on etiquette."[25] Nevertheless, the Chinese Communist Party states that it is maintaining and continuing the revolution and that the People's Republic of China is still socialist.

25   Joseph Kahn, "Where's Mao? Chinese Revise History Books," *New York Times*, September 1, 2006.

Nature and Transformation

"Make the high mountain bow its head; make the river yield its way." It is an excellent sentence. When we ask the high mountain to bow its head, it has to do so! When we ask the river to yield the way, it must yield!

—Mao Zedong in a speech to the Second Session of the Eighth Party Congress, May 1958 [1]

The natural landscape was a favorite subject in traditional Chinese watercolor painting. Delicate clouds, gossamer foliage, and spectacular mountains soothed the eye and uplifted the soul. China is home to significant sites of natural beauty, including the world's second- and third-largest rivers (the Yellow and the Yangtze), the Himalaya mountain range, and scenic coastlines. During the GPCR this genre expanded to include the transformative hand of the Chinese people. It is easy to miss the subtle clues at first glance—but every one of the landscape paintings from this era includes features of human development, such as power lines, agricultural terracing, and soldiers on maneuvers. Historically, China has suffered repeated natural calamities such as floods, earthquakes, and droughts, many with massive loss of life. Efforts to control nature were seen as a survival response, and projects to increase arable land and generate electricity were driven by the desire to improve quality of life. It was only after the GPCR that "pure" nature returned, displaying Chinese pride in the country's varied and beautiful countryside for its own sake.

1 "Speeches at the Second Session of the Eighth Party Congress (8–23 May 1958)," The First Speech. *Miscellany of Mao Zedong Thought (1949–1968), Part I* (Arlington, VA: Joint Publications Research Service, 1974).

风 景 这 边 独 好 （版 画）

The scenery on this side is great.
Artwork by Jiang Xueliang; published by
People's Fine Art Publishing House, 1973.
53 x 39 cm

Top
In praise of Yanan.
Artwork by Qian Songyan; published by
Shanghai Book & Painting Publishing
House, 1976. 77 x 53 cm

Bottom
Grazing in the high mountains.
Artwork by Deng Zijing; published by
People's Fine Art Publishing House, 1973.
39 x 53 cm

Top left
Opening canals in the mountains.
Artwork by Chen Zhongyi; published by
Tianjin People's Fine Art Publishing House,
1973. 76 x 53 cm

Top right
The new look of Longtan.
Artwork by Xu Jialin; published by Ningxia
People's Publishing House, 1972.
77 x 53 cm

Bottom
Dazhai aerial view.
Artwork by Zhang Yuqing; published by
Shanghai People's Publishing House,
1975. 53 x 77 cm

不靠天

Don't depend on the heavens.
Artwork by Xiyang County Amateur Fine
Art Production Group; published by
Shanghai People's Publishing House,
1975. 77 x 53 cm

红 日 照 延 安 〔中国画〕

The Red Sun over Yenan (Chinese traditional painting)
Le soleil rouge illumine Yenan (peinture de style traditionnel)
Hell strahlt die rote Sonne über Yenan (Malerei im traditionellen chinesischen Stil)

The Red Sun over Yanan.
Artist unknown; published by Shanghai
People's Publishing House, 1971.
27 x 37 cm

漓 江 雨 霁

周太阳 作

Mist on the Li River.
Artist unknown; published by Guangxi
People's Publishing House, 1973.
39 x 53 cm

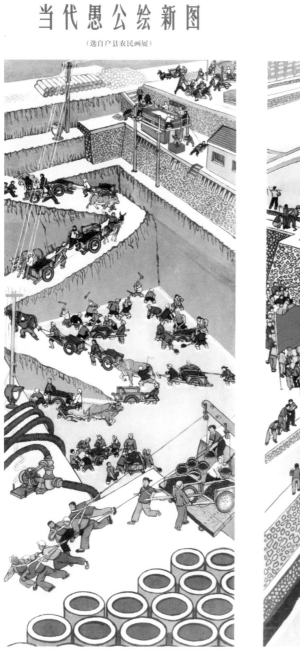

Modern Yu Gongs building the future
[refers to a mythical character known for
persistence].
Selection from Hu County Peasant Painting
Exhibition; publisher unknown, n.d.
77 x 53 cm

山村秋色 （油画）

通途劈上彩云间 （中国画）

Top
Autumn in a mountain village.
Artwork by Lu Ruozeng; published by
People's Fine Art Publishing House, 1973.
38 x 52 cm

Bottom
Broad road to a bright future.
Artwork by Guilin Professional and
Amateur Fine Art Workers; published by
People's Fine Art Publishing House, 1972.
38 x 52 cm

韶　山　（中国画）

Shao Mountain [Mao's birthplace].
Artist unknown; published by Shanghai
People's Publishing House, 1971.
27 x 37 cm

Production and Mechanization

One of the primary tasks of the Chinese revolutionary government was to improve material conditions in this poor, largely agricultural country. Although Mao Zedong viewed some proposed "modernization" models as a "road to capitalistic restoration," this did not mean that efforts to advance the material conditions of the Chinese citizens ceased during the GPCR. The country embarked on a simultaneous development of industry and agriculture, involving both large-scale state-run projects and reliance on coordinated local initiative. The two different but parallel development strategies, known in China as "Walking on Two Legs," are evident in these posters.

Lessons had been learned from what many felt was the overreaching effort toward self-sufficiency promoted by the Great Leap Forward campaign of the late 1950s, and new approaches were implemented for industries that require massive capitalization, such as shipbuilding, mining, steel, and oil exploration run by government planning agencies. The very productive Daqing oilfield in Heilongjiang Province was developed in 1968. However, such industrial output declined overall during the GPCR. Periodically, trains and trucks were deployed to transport political activists rather than produce, operations slowed when managers were subject to criticism campaigns, and many workers were involved in political struggle.

On the other hand, the political component of the GPCR that extolled community service resulted in numerous successful local economic development projects. Communes undertook a remarkable number of public works, including road building, irrigation, and flood control. The Dazhai Production Brigade in Shaanxi Province emerged as a model for the transformative power of local labor projects. This commune had been boosted from impoverished countryside to productive farmland through dedicated political study leading to effective actions arising from collective local effort. Its actions exemplified the practice of putting "politics in command," using revolutionary theory as a concrete basis for action. A significant amount of effort went into preparation for disaster, whether from natural causes or enemy attack. Everyone was encouraged to store food, maintain shelters, and engage in military training in the eventuality of an assault from the Soviet Union or from the United States—dangers that were very real during the heightened military posturing by these countries throughout the Cold War.

Improved infrastructure (roads, electric power, and so on) coupled with locally produced technology was promoted as a national goal. Note the difference between the 1965 poster [see page 56 top right] in which rice is being sown by hand and the 1973 poster [see page 65] showing off the new rice-planting machine.

为实现农业电气化而奋斗

十大路线指航向
满怀豪情夺丰收

加速农业机械化的步伐　为农业现代化而奋斗

Top left
**Work hard for the
electrification of agriculture.**
Artwork by Shanghai Fine Art
Design Company; published by
Shanghai People's Publishing
House, 1972. 106 x 77 cm

Top right
**The Tenth Congress of the CCP
guides us, enthusiastically
strive for a great harvest.**
Artwork by Qu Guhan and
Xi Guorong; published by
Shanghai People's Publishing
House, 1974. 106 x 77 cm

Bottom
**Speed up the mechanization
of agriculture, strive for the
modernization of agriculture.**
Artwork by Liu Wenxi;
published by People's Fine Art
Publishing House, 1975.
77 x 94 cm

Opposite
**Make the great leader
Chairman Mao proud,
make the great socialist
motherland proud.**
Artwork by Central Arts and
Crafts Institute; publisher
unknown, 1970. 106 x 77 cm

为伟大领袖毛主席爭光
为伟大社会主义祖国爭光

亲切的关怀巨大的鼓舞

自力更生 艰苦奋斗 加快社会主义建设

Top
Caring deeply, encouraging diligently.
Artwork by Shanghai Electric Motor
Factory Revolution Committee Political
Campaign Team; published by Shanghai
People's Publishing House, 1971.
77 x 106 cm

Bottom
**Rely on your own strength—struggle
hard, expedite the building of socialism.**
Artwork by Shanghai People's Publishing
House Fine Art Group; published by
Shanghai People's Publishing House,
1973. 106 x 77 cm

Top
Agriculture—learn from Dazhai, work hard to make great changes.
Artwork by Chao Xinlin; published by Henan People's Publishing House, 1975.
77 x 106 cm

Bottom
Work hard and persistently to support agriculture.
Artwork by Yue Xiyan; published by Henan People's Publishing House, 1975.
77 x 106 cm

毛主席和我们心连心

在实际斗争中锻炼
在工农群众中扎根
知识分子劳动化

'IN SHI FEN ZI LAO DONG HUA

Top left
We love Chairman Mao.
Artwork by Han Min; published by
Shanghai People's Fine Art Publishing
House, 1964. 77 x 53 cm

Top right
Intellectuals participate in labor.
Artwork by Ha Qiongwen; published by
Shanghai People's Fine Art Publishing
House, 1965. 77 x 52 cm

Bottom
Work half-time, study half-time.
Artwork by Zhao Zheng, Jin Kequan;
published by People's Fine Art Publishing
House, 1965. 54 x 77 cm

**Struggle for a good harvest and store
food supplies everywhere. [Text on
basket: People's communes are good.]**
Artwork by Shanghai People's Publishing
House Poster Production Group; published
by Shanghai People's Publishing House,
1973. 53 x 77 cm

日 新 月 异 （版画）

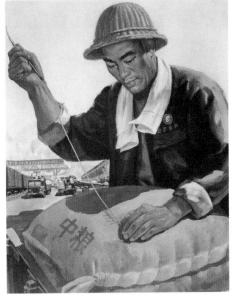

要节约闹革命 一砖一瓦看方向
一针一线为人民

综合利用 大有文章可做
ZONG HE LI YONG DA YOU WEN ZHANG KE ZUO

Bottom left
Hu County peasant revolutionary education painting series (6).
Artwork by Niu Dong Commune Amateur Artists Group; Hu County Peasant Class Education Series published by Shanghai People's Publishing House, 1974. 53 x 39 cm

[with poem:]
The spirits of the sons and daughters of Yanan are very high;
Daring to change mountains and rivers;
Struggling against heaven and earth for good harvests;
Dazhai, like a red flower, blooms everywhere.

Bottom right
Exciting new prospects.
Artwork by Qin Jianming, Yao Yuqi; published by People's Fine Art Publishing House, 1973. 52 x 38 cm

火树银花不夜天 (中国画)

大庆红旗 (中国画)

Top
Firetree silver flower.
Artwork by Zhang Guiming, Yan Guoji, Xu Zhiwen, Cheng Shifa, Xie Zhiguang; published by People's Fine Art Publishing House, 1973. 38 x 53 cm

Bottom
Red flags at Daqing.
Artist unknown; published by People's Fine Art Publishing House, 1977. 38 x 53 cm

Opposite
Another good harvest year.
Artwork by Gu Pan, Pan Honghai; published by People's Fine Art Publishing House, 1972. 77 x 53 cm

又 是 一 个 丰 收 年

THE BRIGADE'S DUCKS   LES CANARDS DE LA BRIGADE DE PRODUCTION   DIE ENTEN DER PRODUKTIONSBRIGADE

Top
The brigade's ducks.
Artist unknown; published by People's Fine
Art Publishing House, 1973. 53 x 77 cm

Bottom left
**The great struggle against crooked
valleys and rivers [Quyu River].**
Artwork by Liu Zhide; published by
Shanghai People Publishing House, 1974.
53 x 77 cm

Bottom right
Nursing baby sheep.
Artwork by Niu Xiwen; published by
Ningxia People's Publishing House, 1973.
53 x 77 cm

工 农 一 家 喜 迎 春

煤 海 盛 开 大 庆 花

Top
**Peasants and workers greeting
the new year.**
Artwork by Fu Qiong, Feng Jianxin;
published by People's Fine Art Publishing
House, 1975. 53 x 77 cm

Bottom
**The spirit of Daqing is blooming
in a coal mine.**
Artwork by Li Yansheng, Huang Huabang,
Ren Guisheng; published by People's Fine
Art Publishing House, 1972. 53 x 38 cm

俺 社 创 造 了 打 井 机

边 疆 新 景 象

Top
Our commune builds well-drilling equipment.
Artwork by Zhang Herong, Cai Xu; published by People's Fine Art Publishing House, 1973. 53 x 77 cm

Bottom
The border's new look.
Artwork by Zhang Yuqing; published by Shanghai People's Publishing House, 1973. 53 x 77 cm

机器插秧好

Planting rice by machine is wonderful.
Artwork by Huang Miaofa; published by
Shanghai People's Publishing House,
1973. 53 x 77 cm

Women Hold Up Half the Sky

Raising the status of women was one of the keystones to the Chinese revolution. Mao Zedong's early writings included essays about the need for gender equality:

> A man in China is usually subjected to the domination of three systems of authority [political authority, clan authority, and religious authority]. . . . As for women, in addition to being dominated by these three systems of authority, they are also dominated by the men (the authority of the husband). These four authorities—political, clan, religious, and masculine—are the embodiment of the whole feudal-patriarchal ideology and system, and are the four thick ropes binding the Chinese people, particularly the peasants. . . .
>
> —Mao Zedong, "Report on an Investigation of the Peasant Movement in Hunan," 1927

The posters of the GPCR reflect this long-term goal of the revolution. The barriers to this struggle were enormous: "second wives," concubines, women who drowned themselves in wells when "disgraced," and the binding of women's feet were still common practices at the time. The Chinese Communist Party organized work among women and called for an increased role for them in production as well as leadership in all aspects of Chinese life. Later, the well-known quote "Women hold up half the sky" was used by Mao Zedong himself. During the GPCR, the spirit of "questioning authority" extended to reexamining the authority of the husband and the father, and women were shown in a wide variety of roles in the revolutionary effort to build a new society.

Left
Always on the go, and knows your heart [Barefoot doctor].
Artwork by Chen Rongqing; published by Shanghai Book & Painting Publishing House, 1977. 77 x 53 cm

Right
Hu County peasant revolutionary education painting series (3).
Artist unknown; publisher unknown, 1974. 53 x 39 cm

[with poem:]
This woman's child starved to death;
She came to the landlord's house alone;
She works like an ox or a horse every day;
Her hatred goes deep in her heart and grows like a seed in the ground.

侗寨妇女 (国画)   周秀清作

Top
Grassland women's militia.
Artwork by Liu Shengzhan; published
by Hebei People's Publishing House, 1973.
53 x 77 cm

Bottom
Tong Zhai women.
Artist unknown; published by Beijing
People's Publishing House, 1972.
26 x 37 cm

Top
Electricity reaches our village.
Artwork by Xu Jiping; published by
Shanghai People's Fine Art Publishing
House, 1965. 53 x 77 cm

Bottom
Two sisters.
Artwork by Wang Zunyi, Ying Peihua;
published by People's Fine Art Publishing
House, 1975. 77 x 53 cm

军民联防
铁壁铜墙

The army and the people guarding the
border together are a wall of iron.
Artwork by Chinese PLA Chengdu District;
published by People's Fine Art Publishing
House, 1971. 77 x 53 cm

大力增产化肥 支援农业生产

为加速实现农业机械化而奋斗

到工农兵群众中去 到火热的斗争中去
Go Among the Workers, Peasants and Soldiers and into the Thick of Struggle!
Allons parmi les ouvriers, paysans et soldats! Jetons-nous dans la lutte ardente!
Unter die Massen der Arbeiter, Bauern und Soldaten gehen, zu flammendem Kampf gehen!

胸怀革命壮志 勇攀世界高峰

Opposite
Work hard to increase the fertilizer production, support agriculture.
Artwork by Shanghai Fine Art Design Company; published by Shanghai People's Publishing House, 1972. 106 x 77 cm

Top
Strive to speed up the mechanization of agriculture.
Artwork by Beijing 76th Middle School Revolution Committee; published by People's Fine Art Publishing House, 1971.
77 x 106 cm

Bottom left
Go among workers, peasants and soldiers and into the thick of struggle!
Artist unknown; published by Shanghai People's Publishing House, n.d. 106 x 77 cm

Bottom right
Have revolutionary aspirations close to your heart. Bravely climb the world's highest peak.
Artwork by Song Huimin; published by People's Sports Publishing House, 1975.
106 x 77 cm

军民团结如一人 试看天下谁能敌

立志做一辈子农民

Top
The army and the people are united as one, let's see our match in the world.
Artist unknown; publisher unknown, circa 1963. 76 x 107 cm

Bottom
Determined to be a lifetime peasant.
Artist unknown; publisher unknown, 1966.
53 x 76 cm

继承革命传统做红色接班人

JI CHENG GE MING CHUAN TONG ZUO HONG SE JIE BAN REN

Continue the revolutionary tradition,
become revolutionary successors.
Artwork by Hang Mingshi; published by
Liaoning Fine Art Publishing House, 1965.
77 x 53 cm

壮 志 凌 云 （油画）

Lofty aspirations touch the clouds.
Artwork by Yuan Hao; published by
People's Fine Art Publishing House, 1973.
36 x 32 cm

光荣人家春更浓

女支书

妇女能顶半边天　管教山河换新颜

Top left
Bringing greater happiness to a Glorious Family.
Artwork by Zhang Boyuan; published by Hebei People's Publishing House, 1974.
77 x 53 cm

Top right
Female artillery soldiers.
Artwork by Li Baijun; publisher unknown, circa 1965.
77 x 53 cm

Bottom left
Female party secretary.
Artwork by Liu Zhide; published by Shanghai People's Publishing House, 1975. 77 x 53 cm

Bottom right
Women hold up half the sky, dare to change the mountains and rivers.
Artwork by Wang Dawei; published by People's Fine Art Publishing House, 1975.
77 x 53 cm

Left
A new soldier for the coal mine.
Artwork by Yang Zhiguang; published by
People's Fine Art Publishing House, 1972.
53 x 38 cm

Right
Whole heart and whole spirit.
Artist unknown; published by Shanghai
People's Publishing House, 1973.
39 x 27 cm

壮 志 凌 云

Sky-high ambitions.
Artwork by Shi Qi; published by
People's Sports Publishing House, 1977.
77 x 53 cm

Serve the People

Role models in various forms were a common vehicle for tangibly expressing the socialist value to "serve the people." One of the principal tenets of the Chinese revolution was that the best way to attain a better society was collectively, not individually, and that guidance for that effort should come from the workers, peasants, and soldiers. Exemplary models could be heroic individuals, meritorious communes, or distinguished events and landmarks. Among individuals, obvious ones were living Chinese revolutionary leaders such as Mao Zedong and Zhou Enlai. During the civil war with the Chinese Nationalist Party (Guomindang) in the 1930s, Communist Party member Liu Hu Lan was executed with butcher knives for refusing to reveal information under torture. Lei Feng was a soldier of the People's Liberation Army whom Mao Zedong promoted as a role model because of his selfless, persistent quest to reduce waste and improve efficiency in personal everyday ways. Wang Jie was in the People's Liberation Army and threw himself on an accidental dynamite explosion in order to save bystanders. Likewise, in 1964 the Dazhai Production Brigade in Shaanxi Province was cited for its extraordinary worker-led success when Mao Zedong called on the people to act on the slogan: "In agriculture, learn from Dazhai." The Long March strategic retreat from the Guomindang to Yanan, where the Red Army made camp from 1937 to 1947, was a model for its role in achieving victory in the Chinese civil war.

Whole categories of the population—workers, peasants, and soldiers—were held up for respect and emulation. Public service was a subject of family and village pride. Children were also encouraged to engage in deeds that benefited their community. Chinese model operas served as dramatic devices for presenting socialist values. Of the thirteen or so operas with revolutionary themes (essentially dramatic ballets with song), eight of the most popular were termed "The Eight Model Works" and were a significant cultural presence during the GPCR. Likewise, by circulating revolutionary culture and educational materials, efforts were made to build respect for people from rural areas and combat the "Four Olds" (old ideas, old culture, old customs, and old habits associated with the oppressors and exploiters from past ruling classes).

During the GPCR, despite an emphasis on Chinese self-reliance and nationalism, some Western values, individuals, and movements were also honored. These included the revolutionary panel of Karl Marx, Friedrich Engels, Vladimir Lenin, and Joseph Stalin, as well as the Paris Commune of 1871 with its revolutionary anthem "The Internationale." (In testament to the enduring spirit of this work produced by a Paris Communard, students and workers sang it at the 1989 Tiananmen Square protests.) Canadian doctor Norman Bethune, highly respected for helping the Chinese during their resistance to Japanese occupation during the late 1930s, served as a model of internationalist selfless service to the people.

兵民是胜利之本

《五·七指示》万岁！

Top
**The soldiers and the people are
the basis of victory.**
Artwork by Beijing 76th Middle School;
publisher unknown, circa 1970.
77 x 106 cm

Bottom
Long Live (May Seventh Instructions).
Artwork by Chinese PLA Chengdu District;
published by People's Fine Art Publishing
House, 1971. 77 x 106 cm

英特纳雄耐尔就一定要实现

纪念无产阶级诗人、《国际歌》作者欧仁·鲍狄埃

团结战斗学大寨　大干大变夺丰收

Top
**Internationalism will certainly
be achieved.**
Artwork by Beijing Fine Art Company
Production Group; published by People's
Fine Art Publishing House, 1972.
77 x 106 cm

Bottom
**Unite and struggle to learn from
Dazhai, work hard and make big changes
to achieve great harvests.**
Artwork by Fu Zhisen; published by
People's Fine Art Publishing House, 1975.
77 x 106 cm

Top left
Learn from the workers, peasants, and soldiers; serve the workers, peasants, and soldiers.
Artwork by Liao Yiqun; published by People's Sports Publishing House, 1974. 106 x 77 cm

Top right
Become a person like this one.
Artwork by Shan Lianxiao; published by People's Fine Art Publishing House, 1972. 106 x 77 cm

Bottom left
Norman Bethune [Mao quote].
Artwork by Chairman Mao Revolutionary Line Triumph Exhibition; published by Shanghai Revolution Education Publishing House, 1968. 77 x 53 cm

[text reads:] "Comrade Bethune's spirit, his utter devotion to others without any thought of self, was shown in his boundless sense of responsibility in his work and his boundless warmheartedness toward all comrades and the people. Every Communist must learn from him."—Mao Zedong

人民送我上大学　我上大学为人民

Opposite, bottom right
Study technology for the revolution.
Meng Xianchang; published by Shanghai
People's Publishing House, 1972.
77 x 53 cm

Top
The people send me to the university,
I go to the university for the people.
Artwork by Yu Dawu; published by
People's Fine Art Publishing House,
1976. 106 x 77 cm

Bottom
Long live Chairman Mao's
revolutionary cultural line.
Artwork by Ding Jiasheng and others;
published by Shanghai People's
Publishing House, 1974. 77 x 106 cm

We should be as brave as Liu Wenxue;
we should be as vigilant as Wen Qinghai.
Artwork by Li Zhonggui; published by
Beijing Publishing House, 1965.
78 x 53 cm

We should love our group like Long Mei
and Yu Rong; we should serve the people
wholeheartedly like uncle Lei Feng.
Artwork by Li Zhonggui; published by
Beijing Publishing House, 1965.
78 x 53 cm

为工农兵服务,同工农兵结合!

学大寨之风 长大寨之志 走大寨之路

向王国福同志学习!

"拉革命车不松套,
一直拉到共产主义"

提高警惕,保卫祖国!
随时准备歼灭入侵之敌!

Heighten our vigilance, defend the motherland! Be ready at all times to destroy the enemy intruders!
Redoublons de vigilance, défendons notre patrie! Soyons toujours prêts à anéantir tout envoyer intrus!
Die Wachsamkeit erhöhen, das Vaterland verteidigen! Jederzeit zur Vernichtung einfallender Feinde bereit!

Top left
Serve the workers, peasants, and soldiers; join the workers, peasants, and soldiers.
Artist unknown; published by People's Fine Art Publishing House, 1972. 77 x 106 cm

Top right
Learn from comrade Liu Yingjun: carry forward the highest instructions.
Artwork by Yin Rongsheng; published by People's Fine Art Publishing House, 1965. 77 x 53 cm

[text on board:] "Chairman Mao Quotation. Be resolute and fear no sacrifice, overcome all difficulties to win victory."—The Old Man Who Moved the Mountain

Bottom left
Learn from Comrade Wang Guofu!
Artist unknown; publisher unknown, 1970. 106 x 77 cm

Opposite bottom right
**Increase alertness, guard
the motherland, be ready at all times to
destroy the enemy intruders.**
Artist unknown; published by Beijing
People's Fine Art Publishing House, 1986.
106 x 77 cm

Above
**Learn Chairman Mao's writings
like comrade Wang Jie: do as
Chairman Mao says.**
Artwork by Ha Qiongwen; published by
Shanghai People's Fine Art Publishing
House, 1965. 78 x 53 cm

革 命 圣 地 —— 延 安

A revered revolutionary place [Yanan].
Artist unknown; published by
People's Fine Art Publishing House,
1971. 53 x 77 cm

革命现代舞剧 白毛女

谁 又 替 我 把 雪 扫

Top
Modern revolutionary dance play:
White Haired Woman.
Artist unknown; published by Shanghai
People's Publishing House, 1972.
53 x 77 cm

Bottom left
Childhood [Rent Collection Courtyard
sculptures].
Artwork by Jia Xingtong; published by
People's Fine Art Publishing House, 1973.
52 x 38 cm

Bottom right
Who cleaned up the snow for me again?
Artwork by Liu Xiaoli; published by
People's Fine Art Publishing House, 1975.
77 x 53 cm

Top
Prime Minister Zhou Enlai.
Artist unknown; published by
Archaeological Heritage Publishing House,
1979. 38 x 50 cm

Bottom
Never stop fighting [Lu Hsun].
Artwork by Tang Xiaoming; published by
People's Fine Art Publishing House, 1973.
38 x 53 cm

Peasant sons.
Artwork by Cai Liang; published by
Changan Fine Art Publishing House, 1965.
65 x 52 cm (folded for hanging)

祖 国 处 处 有 亲 人

向雷锋同志学习
XIANG LEIFENG TONGZHI XUEXI

洪气长存（油画）　　　　　　张合 林如沐

Opposite
A nation of caring people.
Artwork by Zhou Zhenqing,
Wang Ke, Liu Yongle, Yi Jinyu;
published by Beijing People's
Publishing House, 1973.
77 x 53 cm

Top left
Learn from comrade Lei Feng.
Artwork by Wang Lizhi;
published by Shandong
People's Publishing House,
1973. 77 x 53 cm

Top right
**Pride lives forever [Yang
Kaihui, revolutionary martyr,
wife of Chairman Mao].**
Artist unknown; published by
Shanghai People's Publishing
House, 1977. 37 x 26 cm

Bottom
Dazhai red flag.
Artist unknown; published by
People's Fine Art Publishing
House, 1977. 38 x 53 cm

Solidarity

As a leader in what was seen as an international movement against capitalist expansion that knows no national boundaries, the CCP expressed firm solidarity with other revolutionary forces around the world. China assisted the African countries of Tanzania and Zambia, covertly supported the national liberation movement in Indonesia, and backed the Vietnamese in their struggle against the United States. Some otherwise logical choices were awkward because they were aligned with the Soviet Union's camp, which the CCP said was taking a revisionist path deviating from the true direction of Marxism. Although China and Cuba established formal relations soon after Cuba's revolution in 1959, the Soviet Union emerged as the island nation's dominant Socialist Bloc partner. China found itself contesting Soviet internationalism by proxy in several of the African postcolonial revolutionary movements. During the Angolan civil wars following independence from Portugal in 1975, the United States supported the South African–backed National Front for the Liberation of Angola (FNLA), Cuba and the Soviet Union backed the Popular Movement for the Liberation of Angola (MPLA), and China supported the FNLA as well as the National Union for the Total Independence of Angola (UNITA).

China also took a keen interest in the social upheavals occurring in the United States during that period, especially the movement for racial equality. During the GPCR, Red Guards at the Atlas (or Map) Publishing House produced the *Atlas Fighting Paper*, in which maps of world revolutionary hot spots (such as Palestine, Vietnam, Burma, and Paris) were marked with flames. The small, text-rich poster on the United States (see page 99 bottom left) includes Mao Zedong's "Statement in Support of American Black People's Anti-Repression Struggle (April 16, 1968)"

> "Recently, the Black American Martin Luther King was suddenly murdered by American imperialists. Martin Luther King was an advocate of non-violence, but this did not lead the American imperialists to be lenient to him, rather they used counterrevolutionary violence to bloodily suppress him. This was a profound lesson to American Blacks, arousing a new storm of anti-repression struggle unprecedented in American history, engulfing over 100 American cities...."

Expression of solidarity also included Chinese national and ethnic minorities. In 1950, the Chinese government created a program to classify the various minorities within the country, resulting in the official designation of fifty-five nationalities as well as the formation of five autonomous regions. To promote national unity, numerous posters were generated showing unity between the national government and ethnic groups, identified by local costume, cultural activities, and physical characteristics. Finally, the People's Republic of China's long-term interest in reunification with Taiwan and solidarity with the people there constituted another persistent subject.

Top
The evil system of colonialism and imperialism ...
Artist unknown; published by Shanghai People's Fine Art Publishing House, 1968. 77 x 106 cm

Bottom
Smash private ownership.
Handmade print with a group signature block: Beijing Language Institute, Jinggang Mountain [a Red Guard Group]; Red Drawing Soldiers. 34 x 48 cm

Opposite, top left
The Red Sun is in our heart.
Handmade print by Beijing Language Institute student Li Jianping. [Inscribed: To Tang Fandi, from Jianping, Hong Xiao Bing (Red Guard) New Year's Day 1967.] 55 x 40 cm

支援世界人民的反帝斗争!

美国黑人抗暴斗争形势简图

美帝国主义从越南南方滚出去!

Top right
Support the people's anti-imperialist movement across the whole world.
Artwork by You Longgu; published by China Shanghai People's Fine Art Publishing House, n.d. 106 x 77 cm

Bottom left
Annotated map of the situation of black Americans' anti-tyranny struggle.
Artist unknown, Atlas (or Map) Publishing House, 1968.
39 x 26 cm [with self-adhesive strips mounted on back]
[text reads in part:] "A historically unprecedented new storm of anti-tyranny struggle by Black Americans spread with astonishing speed through more than 100 American cities. This makes clear that within the over 20 million Black Americans there is an extremely strong revolutionary force. It has struck a heavy blow to the imperialists who are beset on all sides, at home and abroad..."

Bottom right
American imperialists get out of South Vietnam.
Artwork by Ha Qiongwen; published by China Shanghai People's Fine Art Publishing House, circa 1963.
106 x 77 cm

Top
Resolutely support the anti-imperialist struggle of the Asian, African, and Latin American people.
Artwork by Zhou Ruizhuang; published by Shanghai People's Fine Art Publishing House, 1967. 77 x 106 cm

Bottom
Proletarians of the world, unite!
[background graphic words from *The Internationale*].
Artwork by PLA Pictorial Publishing House; published by People's Fine Art Publishing House, 1971. 106 x 77 cm

Opposite, top
March to victory with Chairman Mao's line on revolutionary culture.
Artist unknown, publisher unknown, 1968. 73 x 156 cm assembled
[composite image of three posters]

沿着毛主席的革命文艺路线胜利前进

马克思主义、列宁主义、毛泽东思想万岁！

一定要解放台湾

We are determined to liberate Taiwan!
Nous libérerons Taiwan!
Wir werden Taiwan unbedingt befreien!

无产阶级专政万岁
纪念巴黎公社一百周年

团结战斗 反帝反霸

Middle left
Long live Marxism, Leninism,
and Mao Zedong Thought!
Artwork by PLA Pictorial
Publishing House; published
by People's Fine Art Publishing
House, 1971. 77 x 106 cm

Middle right
We are determined to
liberate Taiwan!
Artist unknown; published
by Shanghai Publishing
Revolution Group, 1967.
77 x 106 cm

Bottom left
Long live the dictatorship
of the proletariat.
Artwork by Chinese PLA
Airforce Politics Department;
published by People's Fine
Art Publishing House, 1971.
77 x 106 cm

Bottom right
Fight together against
imperialism and tyrants.
Artist unknown; publisher
unknown, 1974. 77 x 106 cm

军民团结一家亲

好歌唱给知心人

Pages 102–103
People all over the world unite to defeat American invaders and their running dogs.
Artwork by Xuhui District House Repairing Company; published by Shanghai People's Publishing House, 1970. 77 x 106 cm

Top
The PLA and the people are united as one family.
Artwork by Qin Dahu; published by Shanghai People's Publishing House, 1973. 53 x 77 cm

Bottom
Singing good songs to people close to our hearts.
Artwork by Zhong Wen; published by Shanghai People's Fine Art Publishing House, 1965. 53 x 77 cm

军民团结 巩固国防

全世界人民反对美帝国主义的斗争必胜

Top
**The army and the people are united
to protect our national boundary.**
Artwork by Zhang Xinguo; published by
Hebei People's Publishing House, 1971.
77 x 53 cm

Bottom
**The fight against U.S. imperialism by the
people of the whole world will succeed!
[composite of two posters].**
Artwork by He Kongde; published by
People's Fine Art Publishing House, 1965.
54 x 155 cm

草 原 长 城

草 原 小 学

为 发 农 业 献 好 马

Top
Great Wall of the Grasslands.
Artwork by Zhang Guanzhe; published
by People's Fine Art Publishing House,
1973. 53 x 77 cm

Bottom left
Grassland elementary school [Mongolia].
Artwork by Ma Zhenxiang; published
by People's Fine Art Publishing House,
1973. 53 x 77 cm

Bottom right
**Contribute more strong horses
to agriculture.**
Artwork by Liu Shengzhan; published
by Hebei People's Publishing House,
1974. 77 x 53 cm

全世界无产者同被压迫人民、被压迫民族联合起来!

QUAN SHI JIE WU CHAN ZHE TONG BEI YA PO REN MIN BEI YA PO MIN ZU LIAN HE QI LAI

全世界劳动人民
大团结万岁

Long Live the Great Unity of the Working People of the World!
Vive la grande unité des peuples travailleurs du monde entier!
¡Viva la gran unidad de los pueblos trabajadores del mundo!

QUAN SHI JIE LAO DONG REN MIN DA TUAN JIE WAN SUI

军民鱼水相依 筑成钢铁长城

JUN MIN YU SHUI XIANG YI ZHU CHENG GANG TIE CHANG CHENG

Top
All proletarians of the world unite with oppressed people and nations.
Artwork by Feng Jianqin; published by Shanghai People's Fine Art Publishing House, 1966. 38 x 107 cm

Middle
Long live the great unity of the working people of the world!
Artwork by Feng Jianqin, Feng Zhi; published by Shanghai People's Publishing House, n.d. 38 x 107 cm

Bottom
The military and the people are as interdependent as fish and water; build a Great Wall of Steel.
Artwork by Dai Hengyang, Lin Cong; published by Shanghai People's Publishing House, 1975. 53 x 77 cm

Politics in Command

Although all of the posters in this book are in some sense "political," the examples in this selection contain overt or subtle messages about the strategic struggles within the CCP. Many use phrases forged in the crucible of revolutionary struggle that might now appear confusing or opaque. Terms such as "dictatorship of the proletariat" are not common outside of socialist countries, and anticommunist perceptions often distort their intended meaning.

One subgroup of posters features events from Chinese and world revolutionary history. These include representations of the feudal conditions before the revolution, the formation of the CCP, the fight against the Japanese invasion, the struggle against the Nationalist Party, the Long March, and the Red Army's stay in Yanan. Some honor heroes of the revolution and promote the study of writings. Finally, they include homage to world revolutionary movements such as the Paris Commune of 1871 and well-known leaders, including Marx and Lenin.

More specific to the GPCR time period were images pertaining to various contemporaneous campaigns and movements. Some of these were:

Criticism of Revisionism (especially in the Soviet Union). Relations with the Soviet Union, strained since the late 1950s, worsened during the GPCR. The CCP position was held that the Soviet leadership had become counterrevolutionary and that capitalism had been restored in the Soviet Union, a precedent the GPCR sought to avoid.

Criticize Lin Biao and Confucius (1974). This was aimed at discrediting Lin Biao by associating his politics with those of the ancient philosopher Confucius, whose writings were interpreted as endorsing slavery, among other things.

Up to the Mountains and Down to the Villages (or Down to the Countryside Movement) (1968–1975). This was a movement that sent urban students and recent graduates to the countryside to live among and learn firsthand from the peasantry and help spread literacy and technical skills. The long-term goals were political education of the urban students and transfer of academic training to the villages, where they were most needed.

把反革命修正主义分子揪出来示众！

无产阶级专政万岁

Long Live the Dictatorship of the Proletariat!

Vive la dictature du prolétariat!

Es lebe die Diktatur des Proletariats!

**Long live the dictatorship
of the proletariat!**
Artist unknown; published by Shanghai
People's Publishing House, n.d.
106 x 77 cm

Opposite, top left
**Make philosophy a sharp weapon in
the hands of the people.**
Artwork by Tianjin Industry Museum
Revolutionary Committee; published
by Tianjin People's Fine Art Publishing
House, 1971. 77 x 106 cm

让哲学变为群众手里的尖锐武器

让哲学变为群众手里的尖锐武器

认真读书 深入批修

煤油灯下刻苦学　继续革命方向明

Top right
Make philosophy a sharp weapon in the hands of the people.
Artwork by Beijing 76th Middle School; published by Beijing People's Publishing House, 1971. 77 x 98 cm

Bottom left
Study carefully, thoroughly criticize revisionism.
Artwork by Beijing Worker Peasant Soldier China Factory; published by Beijing People's Publishing House, 1971. 77 x 100 cm

Bottom right
Study hard by coal oil lamp: get a clear direction for the continuing revolution.
Artwork by Shanghai Security Guard District Amateur Fine Art Production Group; published by Shanghai People's Publishing House, 1973. 77 x 105 cm

深入开展革命大批判

Carry out revolutionary criticism deeply.
Artwork by Beijing Normal Institute,
Revolutionary Culture and Art Department;
published by Beijing People's Publishing
House, 1971. 77 x 101 cm

越学心里越亮堂
YUE XUE XIN LI YUE LIANG TANG

古田会议 (油画)

Top
The more you study, the clearer your mind will be.
Artwork by Lin Longhua; published by
Liaoning Fine Art Publishing House, 1965.
53 x 78 cm

Bottom
Gu Tian meeting.
Artwork by He Kongde; published by
People's Fine Art Publishing House, 1972.
38 x 53 cm

热情支持社会主义新生事物

革命农民运动,好得很!

工业学大庆 普及大庆式企业

Top left
Warmly support new ways of socialism.
Artwork by 37001 Army Politics
Department; published by People's Fine
Art Publishing House, 1977. 77 x 53 cm

Top right
**The peasants' revolutionary
movement is very good.**
Artist unknown; publisher unknown,
circa 1966. 78 x 53 cm

Bottom
**Industry learns from Daqing; make
enterprises like Daqing everywhere.**
Artwork by Liang Yunqing, Shao Jingkun,
Wei Zuyin, Yu Yuechuan; published
by Beijing People's Publishing House,
circa 1977. 53 x 77 cm

Carry the revolution through to the end;
promote the proletariat, eliminate
capitalism.
Artwork by Ha Qiongwen; published by
Shanghai People's Fine Art Publishing
House, 1965. 77 x 53 cm

打好批林批孔的人民战争

工农兵是批林批孔的主力军

Left
Fight well in the peoples' war to criticize Lin Biao and Confucius.
Artwork by Zhang Ruji, Wang Jue; published by People's Fine Art Publishing House, 1974. 77 x 53 cm

Right
Workers, peasants, and soldiers are the main force to criticize Lin Biao and Confucius.
Artwork by Lou Haoben; published by People's Fine Art Publishing House, 1974. 106 x 77 cm

Left
Applying for membership in the Communist Party.
Artwork by Liang Yan; published by People's Fine Art Publishing House, 1974.
53 x 39 cm

Right
Old Party secretary.
Artwork by Liu Zhide of the Hu County Cultural Affairs Office; published by Shaanxi People's Publishing House, 1973.
53 x 39 cm

Left
Hu County peasant revolutionary education painting series (1).
Artist unknown; publisher unknown, 1974. 53 x 39 cm

[with poem:]
Every grain is a drop of blood and sweat;
We are so busy—for whom?
We are completely exploited by the landlords,
Filling us with fury and hatred.

Right
Hu County peasant revolutionary education painting series (2).
Artist unknown; publisher unknown,
1974. 53 x 39 cm

[with poem:]
Pressed into military service
The very poor peasants suffer
Angry eyes dare to stare in defiance.
Someday they will pay for this!

户县农民阶级教育画选 （四）　来了救星共产党，农民翻身得解放。
怒火烧毁卖身契，地主威风一扫光。

Hu County peasant revolutionary education painting series (4).
Artist unknown; publisher unknown, 1974.
53 x 39 cm

[with poem:]
The Communist Party　rescuers arrive;
The peasants are liberated;
The enslaving contract is burned;
The landlord's "glory" entirely disappears.

毛主席和我们心连心

We love Chairman Mao.
Artwork by Shaanxi Fine Art Production
Group; published by People's Fine Art
Publishing House, 1973. 53 x 77 cm

我们心中最红最红的红太阳毛主席万岁！万万岁！

Long live Chairman Mao, the
reddest sun in our hearts; long, long
live Chairman Mao!
Artist unknown; published by Shanghai
People's Fine Art Publishing House, 1967.
19 x 13 cm

Top left
Down with Soviet revisionism!
Artist unknown; published by Shanghai
People's Fine Art Publishing House, 1967.
77 x 53 cm

Top right
**Long live Chairman Mao's
revolutionary cultural line.**
Revolutionary Rebel Headquarters
Fine Art Communication Station;
published by Tianjin People's Fine Art
Publishing House, 1967. 77 x 52 cm

Bottom
We love Chairman Mao.
Handmade print by Beijing Language
Institute artist from "The East is Red"
Red Guard Group; independently
published, 1967. 46 x 62 cm

After the Cultural Revolution

After Mao Zedong's death in 1976 and Deng Xiaoping's return to power in 1977, there was a fundamental reassessment within the CCP about the GPCR. Deep changes in political authority, practices, and policies, which showed up as a distinct shift in the nature of the posters, and issues and personages once shunned began to reappear. A prime example of the "here today, gone tomorrow" quality of Chinese politics at the time is seen by comparing two posters [see page 131, top and bottom] that use a photograph of Mao receiving First Prime Minister Zhou Enlai (with bouquet), along with Party Deputy Chairman Liu Shaoqi (right) and PRC Deputy Chairman Zhu De. In 1966, Liu Shaoqi was removed from the position of CCP deputy chairman, and in 1968 he was expelled from the Party. He died while imprisoned in 1969. In the first poster, from 1977, Liu Shaoqi is not only cropped out; his very existence is airbrushed away. Liu Shaoqi was politically rehabilitated in 1980, an event subtly publicized in the second, unretouched poster.

The "Four Modernizations" era is often described as covering the years 1979–1982, but some consider it began with a proposal raised by Zhou Enlai in 1975[1] calling for a broad series of reforms in the fields of agriculture, industry, national defense, and science and technology before the end of the century. As implemented under Deng Xiaoping, it sought to accelerate economic development and self-reliance through increased international trade, which set the tone for a new phase in mass propaganda. Posters began to display a broader diversity of artistic and design styles—abstraction resurfaced, as did photographic and photorealistic treatments of natural landscapes and "classical"-style illustrations. Equally dramatic was their changed content. A broader range of Western ideas was embraced, as shown by a series of posters featuring influential scientists from all over the world, even the United States and the Soviet Union. There was also a renewed emphasis on classical Chinese history, including scenes from the dynastic past. Images of women were not restricted to representations as workers, peasants, or soldiers, and those that were portrayed as such were more "feminized."

1   "Report on the Work of the Government," Zhou Enlai, First Session of the Fourth National People's Congress of the People's Republic of China, 1975; marxists.org/reference/archive/zhou-enlai/1975/01/13.htm

Opposite
Albert Einstein.
Artwork by Wang Linkun; published by
Shanghai People's Fine Art Publishing
House, 1981. 77 x 53 cm

Left
Charles Darwin [with Lenin quote:]
"Darwin put an end to the belief that
the animal and vegetable species bear
no relation to one another, except by
chance, and that they were created
by God, and hence immutable."
Artwork by Zhou Ruizhuang; published
by Shanghai People's Fine Art Publishing
House, 1981. 77 x 53 cm

Right
Benjamin Franklin.
Artwork by Weng Yizhi; published by
Shanghai People's Fine Art Publishing
House, 1981. 77 x 53 cm

关怀

Left

Liang Hongyu [historical and legendary female general].
Artwork by Hu Yupu; published by Shandong People's Fine Art Publishing House, 1981. 77 x 54 cm

Right

Caring.
Artwork by Liu Wenxi; published by Shanghai Education Publishing House, 1979. 77 x 53 cm

毛主席和周总理、朱委员长在一起

一九六四年十二月，周恩来同志率领中国党政代表团，参加苏联十月社会主义革命四十七周年庆祝活动期间，亲自同访问了苏联数据集团访问波党等国友谊...朴正了马克思主义、列宁主义，周恩来同志从莫斯科回到北京，受到毛主席、朱委员长和首都人民的热烈欢迎。

毛泽东同志、刘少奇同志、周恩来同志、朱德同志在一起。

Top
**Chairman Mao, Prime Minister Zhou,
and Council Chair Zhu together.**
Photographer unknown; published by
Beijing People's Publishing House, 1977.
39 x 53 cm

Bottom
**Comrade Mao Zedong, Comrade Zhou
Enlai, Comrade Liu Shaoqi, and Comrade
Zhu De together.**
Photographer unknown; published by
People's Fine Art Publishing House, 1980.
38 x 53 cm

春　曉

Opposite
Dawn of spring.
Artwork by Jin Hongjun; published by
People's Fine Art Publishing House, 1981.
77 x 53 cm

Bottom left
Playing in springtime.
Artwork by Mao Shuixian; published by
People's Sports Publishing House, 1981.
77 x 53 cm

Top left
Knowledge gives us wings.
Artwork by Tong Zhaohui; published by
Shanghai Education Publishing House, 1980.
77 x 53 cm

Bottom right
Playing the piba by moonlight.
Artwork by Wang Zunyi; published by
Shandong People's Publishing House, 1981.
77 x 53 cm

Top right
Doves.
Artwork by Zou Qikui; published by Tianjin
People's Fine Art Publishing House, 1981.
77 x 53 cm

李時珍
1518—1593
我国的医学家和药物学家·辑成"本草纲目"·书中载有中国药用植物1892种·11000多个单方。

Opposite
Li Shizhen [Chinese naturalist, 1518–1593].
Artwork by Ha Qiongwen; published by Shanghai People's Fine Art Publishing House, 1981. 77 x 53 cm

Above
We Love Socialism.
Artwork by Ha Qiongwen; published by Shanghai People's Fine Art Publishing House, 1983. 77 x 53 cm

翻身农奴热爱华主席 (国画)

**Liberated peasant slaves love
Chairman Hua.**
Artwork by Hua Qimin; published
by Beijing People's Publishing House,
1977. 38 x 53 cm

桂林奇峰烟雨

Gueilin's unique misty mountains.
Artwork by Meng Zi; published by Chinese
Travel Publishing House, 1981. 53 x 77 cm

Bibliography

Posters and Art — Publications

Anchee Min, Duo Duo, and Stefan Landsberger. *Chinese Propaganda Posters*. Cologne: Taschen, 2003.

Andrews, Julia F. *Painters and Politics in the People's Republic of China, 1949–1979*. Berkeley: University of California Press in association with the Center for Chinese Studies, University of Michigan, 1994.

Evans, Harriet, and Stephanie Donald, eds. *Picturing Power in the People's Republic of China: Posters of the Cultural Revolution*. Lanham, Maryland: Rowman & Littlefield, 1999.

Fraser, Stewart E. *100 Great Chinese Posters*. New York: Images Graphiques, 1977.

Graphic Art by Workers in Shanghai, Yangchuan and Luta. Peking, China: Foreign Languages Press, 1976.

Landsberger, Stefan. *Chinese Propaganda Posters: From Revolution to Modernization*. Amsterdam: Pepin Press, 1995.

———. *"To Read Too Many Books Is Harmful" (Mao Zedong): Books in Chinese Propaganda Posters: Objects of Veneration, Subjects of Destruction*. Netherlands: University of Leiden, 2004. An exhibition catalog.

Mao's Graphic Voice: Pictorial Posters from the Cultural Revolution. Madison, Wisconsin: Elvehjem Museum of Art, University of Wisconsin–Madison, 1996. Catalog for an exhibition curated by Patricia Powell, 1996.

Poon, David Jim-tat. "Tatzepao (Wall Poster): Its History and Significance as a Propaganda Medium in Communist China." Master's thesis, University of California at Berkeley, 1969.

Watson, Scott, and Shengtian Zheng. *Art of the Great Proletarian Cultural Revolution, 1966–1976*. Toronto: Morris and Helen Belkin Art Gallery, 2002. An exhibition catalog.

Wilson, William. "A Fascinating Glimpse of China: The Peasant Paintings of Huhsien." *Los Angeles Times Home* magazine, June 18, 1978.

Yanker, Gary. *Prop Art*. New York: Darien House, 1972.

Electronic Resources

Hsiao Min Wang Chinese Poster Art Collection, Claremont Graduate University. www.cgu.edu/pages/3050.asp.

International Institute of Social History (the Netherlands). www.iisg.nl/exhibitions/chairman/chnintro.php.

Jon Sigurdson collection of Chinese posters 1963–1983. Chinaposters.org/front/front.

Picturing Power: Posters of the Cultural Revolution (Centre for the Study of Democracy, University of Westminster, London). Kaladarshan.arts.ohio-state.edu/exhib/poster/PictPow1.html.

GPCR

Cheng, Peter. *A Chronology of the People's Republic of China from October 1, 1949*. Totowa, New Jersey: Rowman and Littlefield, 1972.

Goldwasser, Janet, and Stuart Dowty. *Huan-ying: Workers' China*. New York & London: Monthly Review Press, 1975.

Harris, Nigel. *The Mandate of Heaven: Marx and Mao in Modern China*. London: Quartet, 1978.

Hinton, William. *Hundred Day War: The Cultural Revolution at Tsinghua University*. New York & London: Monthly Review Press, 1972.

Hinton, William. *The Great Reversal: The Privatization of China, 1978–1989*. New York: Monthly Review Press, 1990.

Suyin, Han. *Wind in the Tower: Mao Tse-tung and the Chinese Revolution, 1949–1975*. Boston: Little, Brown & Co., 1976.

Weil, Robert. *Red Cat, White Cat: China and the Contradictions of "Market Socialism."* New York: Monthly Review Press, 1996.

Weil, Robert. "'To Be Attacked by the Enemy is a Good Thing': The Struggle over the Legacy of Mao Zedong and the Chinese Revolution." *Socialism and Democracy*, Vol. 20, No. 2, July 2006, pp. 19–53.

A good physician for the peasants.
Artwork by Liang Hongtao; published by
Shanghai People's Publishing House,
1972. 77 x 53 cm

Index of Posters by Title

Acknowledgments

This book is dedicated to my father, Richard G. Cushing, Associated Press correspondent who covered World War II in the Pacific. He arrived in Shanghai on September 3, 1945, to open the AP bureau, writing about China and Manchuria for more than a year. He never forgot the devastation wrought by the Japanese army and the spirit of the Chinese people in rebuilding a new country. I also wish to thank my family—wife Nina, daughter Ellen, and son Robby—who supported me during my pursuit of this project. —L.C.

To all the Chinese students, colleagues, and numerous Red Guards who welcomed my presence and participation in the Great Proletarian Cultural Revolution, and to Joan Hinton, Sid (Erwin) Engst, Bertha Sneck, the Crook Family, and many other foreign workers resident in China who shared their experience and understanding of China and helped me through the zigs and zags of that historic mass movement. —A.T.

Translations: Yeqiu Wu, friend and colleague; Susan Yan Xue (Electronic Resources Librarian, U.C. Berkeley East Asian Library); Stefan Landsberger; and Mark Hansell (Professor of Chinese, Asian Languages and Literatures Department, Carleton College).

Collection development and editorial support: Terry Ann Rogers, for delivering a requested large order of posters to Ann in the early 1980s; Pam Pierce, Teddy Kell Emrich, Cathryn Fairlee, and Caroline Davis, and several of Ann's friends from or in China—who all gave time and support to various of Ann's drafts; Kathleen Cleaver, Robbin Henderson, Josh McPhee, Steve Louie, Nancy Ippolito, and Peter X. Zhou (director, U.C. Berkeley East Asian Library) for their vibrant oral histories and support for this project; and Michael Rossman, AOUON Poster Archive, Berkeley, for poster research and editorial feedback. Finally, thanks to Kirk Anderson, Cathy Cade, Clifford Harper, Pat Ryan, and Steve Louie for generously contributing their own images to help us better understand the impact of these posters in the United States.

Japanese production poster in demolished forced labor factory, photograph by Richard Cushing, China, 1945.

Technical Note on the Production of this Book

All posters in this book were shot in RAW format with a Kodak DCS Pro SLR-n 13-megapixel camera using a Micro-Nikkor 60mm flat-field lens. Image data went directly to a Macintosh laptop, allowing for color balance control and designated sequential file numbering. The posters were held in place on a wall-mounted 3' x 4' custom-built vacuum copy board, assuring orthogonal flatness without damaging the posters. Lighting was provided by a pair of Lumedyne 200 watt-second electronic strobe units placed at 45° to the copy board. A strobe meter was used to assure even light balance over the image area, with a standard color target and grayscale accompanying each shot. The original RAW format files were saved on DVD and hard drive, then cropped and converted to TIFF format for publication. The resultant files are equal to or larger than 3000 pixels along the longest edge (MOA II guidelines). Tiny poster data type in margins was digitized with an HP Scanjet 4670, which is uniquely designed to facilitate imaging of delicate and oversize documents. Extensis Portfolio, a commercial stock photography application, was used to keep track of images and their relevant data. The search, display, and export functions of the application greatly facilitated the review, selection, and sharing of images.

—L.C.

Building big ships.
Artist unknown; published by Shanghai
People's Fine Art Publishing House, 1963.
77 x 53 cm